anything
with basil

anything green

any
hot fruit

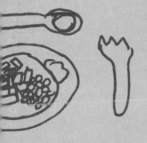

anything which
looks at me

avacado
(you must b joking)

meat that's
not a burger
-takes all Day
to chew

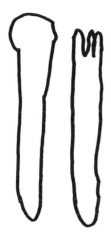

annabel karmel
the fussy eaters' recipe book

120 fast, tasty and healthy recipes to make mealtimes more fun

EBURY
PRESS

This book was inspired by fussy eaters all over the world, not least my children, Nicholas, Lara and Scarlett.

Published in 2007 by Ebury Press, an imprint of Ebury Publishing

3 5 7 9 10 8 6 4

Ebury Publishing is a division of the Random House Group

Text © Annabel Karmel 2007
Photography © Ebury Press 2007

Grace Cheetham's recipes (pages 25 and 155) reproduced by kind permission of Duncan Baird Publishers.

Annabel Karmel has asserted her right under the Copyright, Designs and Patents Act 1988 to be identified as the author of this work.

The Random House Group Limited Reg. No. 954009

Addresses for companies within the Random House Group can be found at www.randomhouse.co.uk

A CIP catalogue record for this book is available from the British Library

The Random House Group makes every effort to ensure that the papers used in our books are made from trees that have been legally sourced from well-managed and credibly certified forests. Our paper procurement policy can be found on www.randomhouse.co.uk

Printed and bound in by Firmengruppe APPL, aprinta druck, Wemding, Germany

Photography: Dave King
Food stylist: Tessa Evelegh
Props stylist: Jo Harris
Copy editor: Helen Armitage

Design: Smith & Gilmour, London

Lettering and illustrations by Charlotte Ottway, India Ottway, Max Ottway and Emily Smith

ISBN 9780091922849

To buy books by your favourite authors and register for offers visit www.rbooks.co.uk

Contents

WHAT'S THE FUSS? Anyone with children will know that when it comes to eating, fuss is often high on the menu. It's not surprising, then that we can lose heart when our children turn their noses up at anything with green bits in, or when they will allow only plain pasta with grated cheese to pass their lips! But rest assured, you're not alone. In fact, 90 per cent of children go through at least one lengthy stage of being fussy. And in a 2007 survey nearly 50 per cent of parents said food is their children's worst area of fussiness, coming well ahead of clothes and even their hairstyles!

In their first year, babies grow more rapidly than at any other time in their life, so it's relatively easy to get them to eat new foods. But by the second year, your child is becoming his or her own person who'll soon figure out that refusing food is a great way of getting attention. Fortunately, nearly all children who have previously been 'good eaters' do go back to eating well. The bad news, though, is that this is usually on their terms – and on their timescale.

WHY FUSS? Children's eating habits have changed dramatically in recent years. Worryingly, more than 25 per cent of children in England are overweight and one in six ten-year-olds is classed as obese. According to a 2007 report, four million people in the UK now suffer from malnutrition, as a direct result of eating more junk food. It doesn't have to be like this for your children.

WAVE GOODBYE TO FUSS! In this book, I have collected together some tasty, quick recipes to tempt the pickiest of eaters, tested by other little fusspots who've given the food the thumbs-up. For confirmed vegetable haters, you'll find cunning ways to hide the 'offending items' in veggie burgers or pasta dishes. Delicious dressings will cajole your child into eating salads and there are even great recipes for making your own healthy 'junk foods' such as chicken nuggets, burgers and pizzas.

I've also included imaginative recipes for crumbles, jellies and ice lollies, all designed to encourage your child to eat more fruit. And there's a whole chapter on gluten-free recipes such as mini polenta pizzas and flourless peanut butter and chocolate chip cookies so children with wheat allergies won't miss out.

By being more responsible and giving children more home-cooked and fresh foods, you will produce meals that are healthy *and* appealing. Lifelong eating habits and tastes are formed in early childhood, and well-stocked kitchen cupboards could be your family's best form of preventive medicine.

Enjoy!

Annabel Karmel

ANNABEL KARMEL

top tips for fussy eaters

be positive 😊

Try to make mealtimes a really positive experience. One of the most important things is to hide your frustration. Praise your child excessively when he or she eats well or tries something new. You may need to ignore some bad eating behaviour to refocus attention on good behaviour. This may make mealtimes less stressful for you, too.

KIDS IN THE KITCHEN Most children adore cooking and tasks such as squeezing fresh orange juice or cracking eggs are well within the capabilities of a young child. It's amazing how being involved in planning and preparing of a meal can stimulate a child's appetite. Cooking is also a great way of bonding with children – spending quality time shopping for ingredients and actually making the recipes together can be a fun task for everyone involved.

It's a good idea to ask your child to invite over a group of friends, choose a menu and get them to prepare their own tea or supper (younger children will need a little adult supervision). Not only are they more likely to eat something they have a hand in preparing – they are also weighing ingredients, measuring time, etc., all without noticing.

It's also fun to organize a cooking birthday party. Sit down with your child and choose a selection of party recipes such as Animal Cupcakes, Pizza Faces, Gingerbread Men and Fruit Kebabs. Group the children in pairs to prepare the food.

I've organized many cooking parties for my children and they were so popular that many of their friends ended up doing the same for their birthdays.

EAT TOGETHER Eating with the whole family whenever possible can really make a difference. Personally, I think that taking the focus off your child's eating and having lots of social chat at the table is helpful. Avoid using mealtimes to assert your authority. If there is a lecture to give, choose another time.

My children are teenagers now and on a Friday night we always try and have dinner together and take it in turns to tell each other some of the good and bad things that happened to us during the week. Sometimes children don't realize that bad things happen to adults, too, so it doesn't matter whether it's trivial or important – dinner time is a time for communicating and getting to know each other. It can soon become a regular family ritual. Children are more likely to open up to you if you are open with them and it's good bonding time.

REWARD SCHEMES In a recent survey 25 per cent of mothers said that they dread mealtimes and nearly 50 per cent admitted they resort to bribery to get their children to eat up. Sticker charts usually work best once your child reaches two and a half. Keep portions absolutely minuscule (he can always ask for more and will get a sense of achievement for finishing his or her meal) and at first give a sticker for just trying the food. Your child could have a yoghurt as a reward for trying his main course. The treats for completing a sticker chart should not be unhealthy foods (e.g. sweets) as this gives the wrong message. Ideally, they should be small and affordable (you may be doing sticker charts for quite a long time!). Make the charts yourself, perhaps using pictures of your child's favourite things (tractors, fairies, etc.) to decorate it. You could even download pictures from the internet for your child to colour in to make the sticker chart with you. Try to keep them short for this age group so that the first one is relatively easily attainable and teaches your child the purpose of these charts.

Another useful reward scheme, for slightly older children, is to fill an empty jar with small objects such as dried pasta shapes. One pasta shape is awarded for eating a meal or trying something new (or any other good behaviour). Start with a small jar and let your child put the pasta in him- or herself. A small present or treat (e.g. family trip to beach/football match/ rollerblading in the park) is the prize for filling the jar so that the lid does not fit on.

Encourage your child to make an 'Eat Up' book. Buy a scrapbook and get your child to stick in the packaging or a photo of the new food that he or she eats. You could find some old food magazines and cut out photos of foods that you would like to get your child to eat and keep them in a shoebox. You could also get your child to draw pictures of the new food. Each time your child has tried or eaten six new foods and stuck them in the book, he or she gets a reward. It might be stickers, jewellery, sports equipment or a trip to the cinema – choose something that would appeal to your child and isn't too expensive.

tea Parties

Invite your child's friends to tea – especially if they are good eaters, so that your child can see his or her friends eating happily. This also helps to keep meals fun and sociable.

dont make a fuss

If your child refuses to eat anything other than junk food, chill out. He or she will soon find there's not much point making a fuss if you don't react.

MAKE FOOD ATTRACTIVE AND FUN
Give small portions – it's not good to overload your child's plate. Also, children generally prefer smaller pieces of food so it's a good idea to make foods such as mini burgers with new potatoes, small broccoli florets and mini carrots. They also like eating from small containers, so use ramekins to prepare individual portions of foods such as fish pie or cottage pie. You can also make a batch and freeze them.

Attractive presentation can make the difference between your child accepting or refusing food. Whole fruit may well not get eaten but thread bite-sized fresh fruit onto skewers or straws and it immediately becomes more appealing.

Children also like to assemble their own food, so you could lay ingredients out in bowls and let your children fill and fold their own wraps or choose their favourite toppings for their home made pizzas.

BLIND MAN'S GRUB If you have a little 'junk food junkie' who refuses to try anything new, play a game in which you blindfold your child and give her several foods to taste, some old favourites and some new, and see if she can identify what they are.

HEALTHY JUNK FOOD Create your own 'healthy junk food'. Make pizza bases using mini muffins, focaccia bread or pitta bread and let your child choose his or her favourite toppings. Make burgers using good-quality lean beef – and I have my own delicious version of chicken nuggets, for which you marinate the chicken in buttermilk, soy sauce, Worcestershire sauce, paprika and lemon and then coat in bread crumbs and Parmesan.

START AS YOU MEAN TO CONTINUE
Start your baby off on fresh baby food rather than jars of processed food with a shelf life of two years. If they are used to a variety of fresh flavours early on, children are much less likely to become fussy eaters when you try to integrate them into family meals.

Once a child's palate has become accustomed to the intense sweetness of refined sugary foods, it is harder for him or her to appreciate the more gentle natural sweetness of fruit. If you want your child to enjoy fresh fruit, restrict sugary foods.

HEALTHY SNACKS After school is a great time to get your child to eat something healthy, as they generally come home starving. The trouble is that most children dive into the biscuit tin or grab a chocolate bar after school. Have something ready prepared on the table. Cut-up fruit on a plate is much more tempting than fruit in a fruit bowl and children like raw veg with a tasty dip. It's quick and easy to make delicious wraps, pitta pockets or pasta salads and it's a good idea to have a low shelf in the fridge from which children can help themselves to tasty healthy snacks.

Reduce snacks between meals to one in the morning and one in the afternoon and make sure they are healthy.

Try to control how much – and what – your child drinks between meals and at meal times. Try to encourage him to drink more water.

YOUR DENTIST IS YOUR ALLY Next time you go, ask the dentist to explain to your child what will happen to his teeth if he eats too many sweets and drinks too many sugary drinks. You can remind him of this the next time he demands the latest sweets and crisps he has seen on TV. Limit sweets to once or twice a week.

LET THEM PACK THEIR OWN LUNCH Get your child involved in packing his own lunchbox – that way you will know what foods he finds acceptable. There are some foods children may eat at home but won't eat in front of friends. Also make sure food is easy and quick to eat. Children won't bother with anything complicated because they are usually in a rush to get to the playground. If you give fruit, it's usually best to cut it up or peel fruits such as clementines and wrap them in cling film.

CHANGE OF SCENERY Take food outdoors in the summer and have a picnic. This could just be in the garden. For some children, a change of scenery works wonders. You could even take teddy bears and spare plates and cups so that the bears can 'eat' with you.

In the summer, barbecues tend to be popular with children – they like hamburgers, drumsticks or corn on the cob cooked on the barbecue.

It's also fun to play make-believe if children are preparing a meal themselves. Let them create a restaurant in one of the rooms in your house– my children used to love doing this: one would be the waiter, the other the chef.

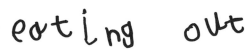 eating out

Watch out for kids' menus in restaurants – they often read like a fast food menu. Ask for a half portion from the adult menu instead. Compliment your child on behaving like a grown-up – children's taste in food is more sophisticated than you might imagine.

variety is the spice of life

Do not just stick to favourite meals. Offer a variety of healthy dishes and keep trying new recipes. Offering only the foods that you are sure your child will eat can encourage extreme fussiness and may lead to a restricted and unbalanced diet.

TRY SOMETHING NEW You are probably frustrated when children refuse to eat something that they have never even tasted. A fear of new foods is known as neophobia. It generally develops at around 18 months and babies who would happily accept many foods suddenly become suspicious and reject anything unfamiliar. If your child has a very restricted diet, it is best to give new foods when she is really hungry, let her see other people eating the same food, try to encourage her to eat just a small amount and give lots of attention and praise if she is willing to try it. If she still refuses to eat it, maybe mix it together with something your child likes. For example, if your child likes pasta but won't eat vegetables, try making a lasagne with spinach.

DON'T BE SCARED OF SAYING 'NO' Children are good at inducing parental guilt but you will make your life difficult if they know that they can twist you around their little fingers. Instead of rewarding good behaviour with sweets or crisps, encourage children to choose treats such as stickers or comics.

PLAY THE FOOD DETECTIVE GAME Make rejecting unhealthy food into a game – ask your child to find a drink that contains less than 10 per cent juice, and then get him to look for one with the words 'pure fruit juice' or '100 per cent juice'. Ask your child to find you a breakfast cereal that isn't high in salt or sugar by picking a cereal with less than 1.25 g salt (0.5 g) sodium or 10 g sugar per 100 g.

If your child pesters you to buy something, ask him to read the ingredients list and if there is a long list of additives that he can't pronounce because he doesn't know what they are, don't buy it.

GIVE YOUR CHILD A CHOICE Talk to your child about what he or she likes and dislikes and what he or she might want for supper in the coming week. Involving your child will lead to less conflict over food.

brilliant
breakfasts

how to get your child to eat a good breakfast

* Try not to buy sugary refined cereals – it's much more difficult to get your child to enjoy healthy cereals once he is used to a sweet taste. Choose instead slow-burning carbohydrates for long-lasting energy, such as Weetabix, muesli, porridge or wholemeal toast.

* A bowl of cereal is a healthy start to the day but you will need to choose carefully. Many cereals aimed at children contain more than 40 per cent sugar. It's easy to make your own fruity muesli or delicious granola (see pages 17 and 19).

* When your child's iron stores are low, less oxygen gets to the brain, resulting in difficulty in concentrating and a shortened attention span. Breakfast cereals are a good source of iron but you need to give your child vitamin C with his cereal – for example, a glass of orange juice or some strawberries or kiwi fruit. You need vitamin C to be able to absorb the iron in the cereal.

* Smoothies are good for breakfast and your child will enjoy making these himself.

* Eggs are good for breakfast – whether it's a scrambled egg, eggy bread or a boiled egg with soldiers.

* Get most of it ready the night before so that you are not stressed in the morning.

* Don't let your child skip breakfast. If your child claims not to be hungry first thing or there is no time to fit in breakfast, think back to the previous evening. When did he last eat and what time did he go to bed? The earlier your child eats and the earlier he goes to bed, the more likely it is that he will fancy food first thing and the easier it will be to get him up 15 minutes earlier.

* Try to eat breakfast with your children if you can.

* A good breakfast should contain some protein (e.g. eggs, cheese or yoghurt, wholegrain cereal or bread and some fresh fruit).

* Be flexible – my children have been known to eat odd things for breakfast such as mini muffin pizzas or tomato soup. Something from last night's dinner might tempt them more than a bowl of cereal. As long as it's nutritious it doesn't really matter what it is.

* If your child has to get to school early and just doesn't have time for breakfast, you can make delicious fruity muffins that he could eat on his way to school with a fruit smoothie.

fruity muesli

A Swiss-style muesli is a good way to encourage a child to eat oats, especially if they are not keen on 'gloopy' porridge. If your child is particularly fussy then try substituting her favourite fruit yoghurt instead of the natural yoghurt.

3 tbsp rolled oats
2 tbsp orange juice or apple juice
2 tbsp natural yoghurt
½ small apple, cored and grated
1 tbsp milk
1 tsp clear honey

SUGGESTED TOPPINGS

APRICOT AND STRAWBERRY
2 ready-to-eat dried apricots, chopped
2 strawberries, quartered

GRAPE AND BLUEBERRY
3 seedless grapes, halved
1 tbsp blueberries

PEACH
1 juicy ripe peach, skinned and chopped

* Soak the oats overnight in a mixture of orange juice or apple juice and yoghurt.
* In the morning, stir in the grated apple, milk and honey. Then add fruits of your choice.

☆ The best way to deliver long-lasting energy in the morning is to give your child complex carbohydrates such as wholemeal bread, or wholegrain cereals such as oats and fruit. The fibre contained in these foods helps slow down the rate at which sugar is released, giving increased concentration and sustained energy. It's easy to make your own delicious mueslis by soaking oats overnight and then mixing in fruits of your choice in the morning.

annabel's granola

This delicious granola is very versatile. You can have it for breakfast with milk. It's also very good on its own as a snack or layered with yoghurt, honey and fruit. If your child is anti-nuts or allergic then you could substitute pumpkin seeds instead, or double the quantity of raisins.

175 g (6 oz) rolled oats
70 g (2½ oz) coarsely chopped pecans
20 g (¾ oz) shredded/desiccated coconut
¼ tsp salt
60 g (2½ oz) soft brown sugar
2 tbsp canola or sunflower oil
4 tbsp maple syrup
50 g (1¾ oz) raisins

* Pre-heat the oven to 150°C/300°F/Gas 2. Put the oats, pecans, coconut, salt and sugar in a large bowl and mix with a wooden spoon.
* Whisk the oil and maple syrup together in a jug or small bowl. Pour over the oats and mix well.
* Spread out on a lightly oiled baking sheet and bake in the centre of the oven for 40–45 minutes, stirring every 10 minutes.
* Transfer to a bowl, stir in the raisins and leave to cool.

☆ Wholegrain cereals are a good source of iron. However, it is difficult for our bodies to absorb iron from a non-meat source (red meat provides the most easily absorbed form of iron). To improve the absorption of iron from breakfast cereal you need to give your child vitamin-C-rich fruit, such as kiwi or berry fruits, or vitamin-C-rich juice, such as orange or cranberry juice.

almost instant porridge

Soaking the oats overnight speeds up the cooking time and makes this a fast but very nutritious breakfast. Fussy eaters should be tempted by one of the delicious toppings.

3 tbsp rolled oats
150 ml (5 fl oz) milk

* Soak the oats overnight in the milk.
* In the morning, put in a microwaveable bowl and cook for 1 minute on high. Stir, then cook for 30 seconds until just boiling (lower-wattage microwaves may need 30 seconds more). Stir again, thoroughly, and allow to cool slightly before serving. (Remember that more than one portion will take longer to cook.)
* Alternatively, transfer the oats to a pan and bring to the boil, stirring. Allow to cool slightly before serving.

SUGGESTED TOPPINGS

BANANA AND MAPLE SYRUP
½ small banana, sliced
2 tsp maple syrup

APPLE, CINNAMON AND RAISIN
a generous knob of butter
1 small dessert apple, peeled and chopped
1 tbsp raisins
2 tsp soft light brown sugar
a pinch of ground cinnamon
* Melt the butter in a pan and sauté the chopped apple with the raisins, brown sugar and cinnamon for 2–3 minutes.

APRICOT AND HONEY
3 ready-to-eat dried apricots, diced
1–2 tsp clear honey

CRUNCHY STRAWBERRY
2–3 strawberries, diced
1–2 tsp demerara sugar

pancake omelette

A thin omelette can be a less challenging way for children to eat eggs in the morning, particularly if you add some of their favourite fillings.

1 large egg
2 tbsp milk
1 tsp butter
a small handful of grated Cheddar
salt and pepper, to season

* Beat the egg and milk together thoroughly with a little salt and pepper.
* Warm a 20-cm (8-in) non-stick frying pan over a medium heat, add the butter and, once melted, pour in the egg mixture and swirl to cover the base. Cook for about a minute until starting to set. Sprinkle over cheese and filling of your choice (see below). Cook for a further 2 minutes, then slip on to a plate and carefully roll up.

SUGGESTED FILLINGS
½ large tomato, seeded and diced
1 small spring onion, sliced
3 mushrooms, sliced and sautéed in 1 tsp butter or oil
crumbled rasher of cooked bacon
1 slice ham, diced (and optional ½ tomato)
30 g (1 oz) cooked chicken, chopped, and ½ diced tomato
2 tbsp drained canned sweetcorn, ½ tomato and a small spring onion, sliced
1 tbsp red pepper, finely diced
1 slice smoked salmon, cut into thin strips
2 tbsp warmed baked beans

☆ A list of the nutritional content of eggs reads like a *Who's Who* of healthy nutrients. They are rich in protein and zinc and vitamins A, D, E and B12 (the latter is essential for vegetarians, as eggs are one of the few non-meat sources of this vitamin). Egg yolks contain lecithin, thought to be an important 'brain food', contributing to memory and concentration. The yolks also contain iron, which is vital for good brain function.

i don't like...

milk unless
it's a chocolate
milkshake

berry burst

Most children love summer fruits, but if they find the seeds off-putting then pass the blended smoothie through a sieve before serving.

85 g (3 oz) fresh or frozen summer berries
1 small banana, peeled and cut into chunks
3 tbsp strawberry yoghurt
2 tsp clear honey
4 tbsp cold milk

* If using frozen fruits, leave them to defrost for about 20 minutes. Put the banana, fruit/berries, yoghurt and honey into a blender and whiz for 1–2 minutes, until smooth. Add the milk and whiz again until frothy.
* Pour into a glass to serve.

sunshine smoothie

This smoothie is a great way to use up slightly overripe bananas – the ones with brown spots that children hate to eat.

1 medium banana, peeled and cut into chunks
½ large mango, cubed
1 tsp clear honey
120 ml (4 fl oz) pineapple juice
60 ml (2 fl oz) orange juice

* Put the banana, mango and honey into a blender and whiz for 1–2 minutes, until smooth. Add the pineapple juice and orange juice and whiz again until frothy.
* Pour into a glass to serve.

Strawberries 😊 and cream

TIP:
Smoothies are a great way not only to tempt a fussy eater to have a nutritious breakfast but also to hide the fact that you are giving them a couple of portions of fruit!

strawberries & cream

The cream soda adds a delicious flavour to this smoothie. It's one of my favourites.

1 medium banana, peeled and cut into chunks
5–8 medium strawberries, hulled and halved
3 tbsp strawberry yoghurt
4 tbsp cream soda

* Put the banana, strawberries and yoghurt into a blender and whiz for 1–2 minutes, until smooth. Add cream soda and whiz again until frothy.
* Pour into a glass to serve.

bananarama

For a banana split smoothie, use chocolate syrup instead of maple syrup. You could use all milk if you prefer.

1 medium banana, peeled and cut into chunks
3 tbsp vanilla yoghurt
1 tbsp maple syrup
4 tbsp apple juice
2 tbsp cold milk

* Put the banana, yoghurt and maple syrup into a blender and whiz for 1–2 minutes, until smooth. Add apple juice and milk and whiz again until frothy.
* Pour into a glass to serve.

grace's dairy-free summer berry smoothie

Tofu is soya beancurd made from soya milk. It provides a good source of calcium so adding it to smoothies if your child has a cow's milk allergy is a good idea. There are two types of tofu – firm tofu and the silken tofu that I have used in this recipe.

500 g (1 lb 2 oz) fresh or frozen summer berries
75 g (2½ oz) silken tofu, cut into small chunks
500 ml (18 fl oz) soya milk
1–2 tbsp clear honey

* If using frozen berries, leave them to defrost for about 20 minutes. Put all the berries into a blender. Add the tofu, soya milk and honey to taste and blend until smooth and creamy.
* Pour into a glass and serve immediately.

french toast with caramelized apples

Challah, a plaited Jewish yeast bread made with eggs and butter, is traditionally served on Friday night in Jewish households, and is good for making French toast. Use slightly stale challah, or brioche is a good alternative. Instead of caramelized apples, try blueberry compote. Put 100 g blueberries in a pan, add 1 tablespoon of caster sugar and a squeeze of lemon juice. Heat gently until the blueberries pop open and release their juices, and then simmer for 2–3 minutes.

CARAMELIZED APPLES

20 g (¾ oz) unsalted butter

2 tbsp caster sugar

2 medium apples, peeled, cored and cut into 12 wedges

FRENCH TOAST

2 thick slices slightly stale white bread, crusts removed

2 eggs

2 tbsp milk

1 tbsp caster sugar

3–4 drops vanilla essence

a knob of butter, for frying

a pinch of ground cinnamon, for sprinkling

* Melt the butter in a frying pan over a medium heat. Stir in the sugar until dissolved. Add the apple slices and, turning them occasionally, cook for 5–10 minutes or until soft and just turning golden.

* Cut the bread into fun shapes like animals or hearts (using cookie cutters), fingers or triangles. Beat the eggs with the milk, half a tablespoon of the caster sugar and the vanilla essence and pour into a shallow dish. Heat a frying pan over medium heat and add the knob of butter. Dip the bread into the beaten egg, making sure that it is thoroughly soaked, then fry each piece for 2–3 minutes or until golden on one side, then flip over and cook for another 2–3 minutes.

* Mix the remaining sugar and the cinnamon together and sprinkle over the hot French toast. Serve the caramelized apples on the side.

my favourite pancakes

Pancakes for breakfast are a real treat and you can make delicious, really thin pancakes with this foolproof batter. Sprinkle them with fresh lemon juice and dust with icing sugar or serve with maple syrup and perhaps some fresh fruit. These pancakes would also make a wonderful dessert or tea-time treat.

120 g (4 oz) plain flour
a generous pinch of salt
2 large eggs
210 ml (7 fl oz) milk
90 ml (3 fl oz) water
60 g (2 oz) butter

* You will need a heavy-based 18-cm (7-in) crêpe pan.
* Sift the flour and salt into a large mixing bowl. Make a well in the centre and crack in the eggs. Beat them into the flour using a whisk or a wooden spoon.
* In a separate bowl mix the milk and water, then gradually beat this into the egg-and-flour mixture until the batter is smooth with the consistency of cream.
* Melt the butter and stir 2 tablespoons of it into the batter. Pour the remaining butter into a bowl. Scrunch up some kitchen paper and dip it into the butter.
* Use the buttery paper to smear the base of the crêpe pan. Always get the pan really hot before pouring in the batter and then turn down the heat to medium. If the first pancake sticks, it's because the pan isn't hot enough. You will need about 2 tablespoons of batter for each pancake and it is a good idea to pour this into a ladle so that it goes into the pan in one go. Tilt the pan quickly until the base is covered with a thin layer of batter.
* Cook over a moderate heat for about a minute until you can see the pan through the batter and the edges begin to lift. Slide a palette knife under the pancake and flip it over. Cook the second side for about 30 seconds. The first side of the pancake should have a pretty lacy pattern, while the second side will be spotted with brown. Serve the pancakes folded with the lacy side out and one of your favourite toppings and fillings (see opposite).
* Wipe the pan with the re-dipped buttery paper before adding the next lot of batter.

FAVOURITE PANCAKE TOPPINGS AND FILLINGS

LEMON AND SUGAR The classic fresh lemon juice-and-sugar combination is hard to beat. Squeeze over some fresh lemon juice and a sprinkling of caster sugar and then fold in half.

CHOCOLATE For chocolate lovers, smooth melted chocolate or chocolate spread over the pancakes. It's also good to add peeled chopped pears. Fold pancakes over and then drizzle with some ready-made chocolate sauce.

PEACH MELBA Spread each pancake with a little strawberry or raspberry jam, add a few chopped well-drained canned or fresh peach slices and fold pancakes in half. Top with a scoop of vanilla ice cream.

MAPLE/GOLDEN SYRUP Pancakes topped with a scoop of vanilla ice cream and then drizzled with warm maple syrup are delicious.

CARAMELIZED APPLE Use recipe for Apples with Toffee Sauce (page 203).

TOFFEE BANANA
50 g (2 oz) butter
50 g (2 oz) light brown sugar
50 ml (2 fl oz) double cream
2 tbsp golden syrup
4 small bananas, sliced
vanilla ice cream, to serve

* To make the toffee sauce, place the butter, sugar, cream and golden syrup in a pan. Heat gently until melted, then bring to the boil and bubble for 1 minute. Spoon some sliced banana on to one side of the pancake, drizzle over some of the sauce, fold in half and then spoon over some more of the toffee sauce and top with vanilla ice cream.

☆ You can make the pancakes in advance and freeze them or store them in the fridge for a couple of days, interleaved with greaseproof paper and covered with cling film. To reheat, pre-heat the oven to 180°C/350°F/Gas 4. Stack the pancakes on a heatproof plate and cover with foil. Warm in the oven for 10–15 minutes. To microwave, stack, cover with cling film, pierce the film and reheat on high for 1 minute. You will need to increase these times if reheating from frozen.

raisin bran breakfast muffins

Muffins are good as you can take them with you if you got up late and didn't have time for breakfast. I have used wholemeal flour to maximize the fibre content in these muffins, but feel free to use half wholemeal and half plain if you prefer (reduce the milk by a couple of tablespoons).

100 g (3½ oz) bran-flake cereal
250 ml (9 fl oz) milk, warmed
125 g (4½ oz) wholemeal flour
2 tsp baking powder
¼ tsp salt
1 tsp ground cinnamon
½ tsp ground ginger
75 g (2½ oz) raisins
1 large egg
100 g (3½ oz) soft dark-brown sugar
100 ml (3½ fl oz) sunflower oil
2 tbsp demerara sugar

* Pre-heat the oven to 200°C/400°F/Gas 6.
* Line a muffin tin with 8 paper cases. Put the cereal in a bowl with the milk and leave to stand for 5 minutes, until the cereal is soft (this can sit while you weigh out the other ingredients).
* Sift the flour, baking powder, salt and spices into a large bowl. Reserve the bran left in the sieve. Stir in the raisins. Beat together the egg, dark-brown sugar and oil and add to the flour mixture, along with the soaked cereal and any milk left in the bowl. Mix.
* Spoon the batter into the muffin cases (fill to the top). Mix the reserved bran from the sieve with the demerara sugar and sprinkle over the muffins. Bake for 20–25 minutes until risen and firm to the touch. Cool for 5 minutes in the tin, then transfer to a wire rack to cool completely.
* Store in an airtight tin for up to five days.

breakfast on the go

It is easy to skip breakfast if you are in a hurry, but here are some portable options that can be eaten on the go. Pack a wet wipe to clean up sticky fingers!

SMOOTHIES in plastic cups with screw-top lids – insulated coffee cups are ideal. Shake well before drinking.

GRANOLA Alternate layers of granola and fresh fruit; place in a plastic tub with a tight-fitting lid. Remember to pack a spoon.

FRUIT DIPPERS Core an apple and cut into 8 wedges. Pack in a plastic sandwich bag with a small tub of yoghurt or fromage frais. Dip the apple in the yoghurt.

FRUIT WRAP Spread 1½ tablespoons full-fat soft cheese over a tortilla and drizzle over 1 tsp clear honey. Put ½ sliced banana at one end along with a few blueberries or a couple of sliced strawberries or a tablespoon of diced mango. Roll up and wrap in foil. The foil can be peeled off as your child eats the wrap. This filling is also good in a sandwich made with granary bread.

BREAKFAST WRAP Melt 2 teaspoons of butter in a small pan. Beat 2 eggs with 1 tablespoon of milk and a little salt and pepper and add to the pan. Cook, stirring over a low heat until the egg has scrambled. Add any of the following to the scrambled egg: ham, bacon, grated cheese, chopped tomato, smoked salmon, sautéed diced sweet pepper and onion plus a few drops of Tabasco. Pile on to one side of a tortilla and roll up. Wrap in foil. The foil can be peeled off as your child eats the wrap.

FRUIT MUFFINS are perfect for eating on your way to school, as are the Raisin Bran Muffins (page 30), Jamaican Banana Muffins (page 181) and the Oat, Apple and Sunflower Seed Muffins (page 183).

i don't like...

egg
any way at all
☹

Not so yucky veg

how to get your child to eat vegetables

* Offer crudités. Many children who don't like cooked vegetables will eat them raw. Vegetables such as carrot, cucumber and sweet pepper sticks make great snacks any time of the day and you can serve them with tasty dip like hummus.

* Disguise vegetables by blending them into a tomato sauce and serve with pasta. You can double-bluff by leaving a few chunky vegetables in the sauce for your child to pick out, then he'll never suspect that there are still some in there.

* Overcooked soggy vegetables are a turn off. Steam rather than boil vegetables: they taste and look better. Alternatively stir fry vegetables. It's worth buying a wok – stir frying mange tout in a little butter is much nicer than boiling them.

* You can sneak vegetables into other popular dishes such as wraps, cannelloni, lasagne, quesadillas or hide vegetables under grated cheese in pizzas.

* A simple batter can transform vegetables into an exciting snack. If you can't get your child to eat any green vegetables, try making courgette batons with a crispy coating flavoured with Parmesan. How about growing your own vegetables and getting your child involved? It's surprisingly easy to grow vegetables such as potatoes, broccoli, courgettes and runner beans. Children will be intrigued to eat something they have grown themselves.

* Instead of boring mashed potato, why not combine mashed potato with carrot or sweet potato – it's a good source of betacarotene. Sweet potato is also delicious on its own and contains more vitamins and fibre than ordinary potato. You can use it as a substitute for potato to make oven-baked potato wedges or mash. Interestingly, the more colourful the vegetable the better it is for you as the pigment contains valuable antioxidants.

* The secret to getting your child to enjoy eating salad is to come up with a delicious dressing. There are some yummy dressings in this book and clever ways with salads like adding crispy noodles or giving the salad a Japanese flavour by adding mirin, soy sauce, rice wine vinegar and honey.

* Try adding some more unusual vegetables like Chinese cabbage, snow peas, bean sprouts and baby sweetcorn to stir fries. Add a splash of teriyaki sauce and some noodles for added child appeal. And how about some child-friendly chopsticks that are joined at the top – your child will have so much fun picking up the food he will forget to make a fuss.

* Children like eating with their fingers so serve vegetables such as whole corn on the cob with melted butter or baked potato wedges.

butternut squash risotto

Rice and pasta dishes tend to be popular with fussy children, so it's a good idea to combine these with nutritious ingredients. Butternut squash is very rich in vitamin A, which is important for healthy skin, eyesight and fighting infection.

1 medium butternut squash, peeled, seeded and cut into 1 cm (½ in) cubes
2 tbsp olive oil
30 g (1 oz) butter
1 large shallot or small onion, diced
1 garlic clove, crushed
200 g (7 oz) risotto rice
1.25 litres (2 pints) hot vegetable or chicken stock
4 tbsp freshly grated Parmesan, plus extra to serve
1 tbsp double cream
salt and pepper, to season
½ tbsp chopped fresh parsley or a little fresh sage (optional), to serve

* Pre-heat oven to 200°C/400°F/Gas 6.
* Toss the squash in the oil and a little salt and pepper, then spread out on a non-stick baking sheet. Roast for 20 minutes, turning halfway through.
* Melt the butter and gently cook the shallot or onion for 5 minutes, until soft but not coloured. Add the garlic and rice and cook for 2 minutes, until the rice starts to turn translucent. Add 300 ml (10 fl oz) of the hot stock (keeping the stock hot throughout) and bring up to a simmer, stirring. Leave to cook for 5 minutes then add another 300 ml (10 fl oz) stock and stir well. Simmer for a further 5 minutes then add another 300 ml (10 fl oz) stock and stir well again. Simmer for a further 8–10 minutes, until the rice is tender.
* Add the roasted squash and Parmesan with another 100 ml (3½ fl oz) stock and cook, stirring, for another 2 minutes. Stir in the double cream and a little of the remaining stock, if needed, to give a loose but not sloppy consistency.
* Remove from the heat and season to taste with salt and pepper. Serve sprinkled with the parsley and extra grated Parmesan.

yummy vegetable and cashew nut burgers

Nuts contain high amounts of protein and, although children can be a little fussy about them, the flavour of the roasted nuts hidden in these burgers should tempt them. Alternatively leave out the nuts and you still get a delicious, nutty flavour from the brown rice.

100 g (3½ oz) unsalted cashew nuts, roasted in the oven
1 tbsp olive oil
1 red onion, chopped
1 carrot, grated
½ small leek, chopped
100 g (3½ oz) mushrooms, sliced
1 garlic clove, crushed
¼ tsp fresh thyme leaves
100 g (3½ oz) cooked brown rice (50 g/2 oz uncooked)
1 tbsp dark soy sauce
40 g (1½ oz) Gruyère, grated
50 g (2 oz) fresh breadcrumbs
1 tbsp clear honey
1 egg yolk
flour, for dusting
2 tbsp sunflower oil, for frying

* Pre-heat the oven to 180°C/350°F/Gas 4. Spread the cashew nuts on a baking sheet and cook for 8–10 minutes. Watch carefully as after about 5 minutes the nuts brown quickly. Alternatively, buy roasted, unsalted cashew nuts.
* Heat the olive oil in a large frying pan with the onion, carrot, leek, mushrooms, garlic and thyme. Sauté for 10 minutes until the vegetables are soft and the liquid has evaporated. Add the rice and cook for 1 minute. Allow to cool slightly.
* Put the cashews in a food processor and pulse 6–7 times, until coarsely chopped. Add the rice mixture and the soy sauce, Gruyère, breadcrumbs, honey and egg yolk with some seasoning and pulse 5–6 times until just combined.
* Form into 8 patties with flour-dusted hands (mixture is a bit wet). Refrigerate for a minimum of an hour or overnight. Heat the sunflower oil in a non-stick frying pan, dust burgers with flour and gently fry for about 3 minutes each side.

annabel's mini vegetable burgers

Getting your child to eat vegetables isn't easy, but turning veg into a burger makes life a lot easier. Mushrooms, carrots, leek and onion all disappear into these burgers. The soy sauce, honey, Gruyère and cayenne pepper add to the delicious flavour. These burgers freeze very well, too, on a tray lined with cling film. Once they are frozen, you can wrap each one individually so that you can remove as many as you need at any time.

1 medium/large potato (approx. 150 g/5½ oz)
2 tbsp olive oil
1 small red onion, chopped
1 medium carrot, grated
¼ leek, finely chopped
50 g (2 oz) brown cap mushrooms, chopped
½ tsp fresh thyme leaves
1 garlic clove, crushed
70g (2½ oz) Gruyère, grated
25g (1 oz) fresh breadcrumbs
½ tsp Worcestershire sauce
1 tbsp dark soy sauce
1 egg yolk
¾ tbsp clear honey
a large pinch cayenne pepper
salt and freshly ground black pepper, to season
COATING
3 tbsp plain flour
1 egg, beaten
90 g (3 oz) fresh white breadcrumbs (approx. 2 slices of bread)
sunflower oil, for sautéeing

* Boil the potato, unpeeled, in lightly salted water until tender (approximately 25 minutes).
* Drain and, when cool enough to handle, peel and grate into a large bowl.
* Meanwhile, put the olive oil in a large non-stick frying pan. Sauté the onion for 3 minutes, then add the carrot, leek, mushrooms, thyme and garlic and cook for a further 10 minutes. Cool slightly.
* Add the vegetables to the grated potato. Mix in the cheese, breadcrumbs, Worcestershire sauce, soy sauce, egg yolk and honey, and season to taste with salt, pepper and cayenne pepper. Form into 12 small burgers. Coat each burger with flour, dip into beaten egg and then in breadcrumbs.
* In a large frying pan, heat the sunflower oil. Sauté as many burgers as will comfortably fit in the pan, flipping at least once, until they are golden on both sides.

focaccia pizza

Pizza tends to be popular even with fussy kids, so try adding some extra toppings such as vegetables or cooked chicken. Once these are covered by the layer of cheese, your child might be more willing to accept them.

9 cm (3 in) focaccia square, split in half
2–3 toppings (see suggested toppings overleaf)
50 g (2 oz) Cheddar or mozzarella, grated
FOR THE SAUCE
1 tsp olive oil
½ red onion, chopped
1 tbsp tomato purée
2 tsp sun-dried tomato pesto
1 tbsp water
salt and freshly ground black pepper, to taste

∗ Pre-heat the grill to high. To make the sauce, heat the olive oil and sauté the onion for 5 minutes. Remove from the heat, stir in the tomato purée, pesto and water and season to taste with salt and pepper.
∗ Put the two halves of the focaccia on a baking sheet cut-side up. Spread over the sauce and add the toppings. Scatter over the cheese.
∗ Grill the pizzas for 4 minutes until the cheese is bubbling and golden. Transfer to plates using a fish slice. Allow to cool slightly before serving.

☆ Focaccia is popular in Italy. The olive-oil-enriched dough used to make the bread is similar to pizza dough and makes a tasty base for a quick pizza. If using unbaked focaccia, split it unbaked, add the topping and bake for approximately 8–10 minutes at 200°C/400°F/Gas 6. Other good bases for making your own pizzas are split and toasted muffins or 12-cm (5-in) lengths of baguette, halved.

focaccia pizza

SUGGESTED TOPPINGS (ENOUGH FOR 2 PIZZAS)

2 tbsp drained canned sweetcorn
2 slices wafer-thin ham, cut into strips
2 handfuls diced chorizo, salami & pepperoni
2–3 mushrooms, sliced and sautéed in 1 tsp olive oil
1 ring pineapple, diced
¼ red or yellow pepper, diced
2 spring onions, thinly sliced
4 slices tomato
4 stoned black olives, thinly sliced
30 g (1 oz) cooked chicken, diced
roasted or stir-fried mixed Mediterranean vegetables
(e.g. sliced courgette, red onion, aubergine, tomato, pepper)
4 sunblush tomatoes, diced (available at the deli counter
of large supermarkets)
2 rashers cooked bacon, crumbled

annabel's secret tomato sauce

Shh... Don't tell anyone! There are five vegetables hiding inside this super-tasty tomato sauce.

1 tbsp olive oil
1 small red onion, chopped
½ leek, finely chopped
1 garlic clove, crushed
¼ red pepper
½ medium carrot, peeled and chopped
½ medium courgette, chopped
400 g can chopped tomatoes
150 ml (5 fl oz) vegetable stock
1½ tbsp tomato purée
1½ tbsp sun-dried tomato paste
1 tsp caster sugar
1 tbsp torn basil leaves (optional)
salt and freshly ground black pepper, to season

* Heat the oil in a pan and sauté the onion and leek for approximately 3 minutes, stirring occasionally. Add the garlic and sauté for 1 minute. Add the red pepper, carrot and courgette, and cook for a further 3 minutes, stirring occasionally. Add the tomatoes, stock, tomato purée and paste and caster sugar, and stir for approximately 1 minute. Simmer uncovered for 25–30 minutes, stirring occasionally until thickened. Stir in the basil leaves if using. Transfer to a blender and blitz the sauce to a purée. Season to taste with salt and pepper.

cheesey courgette batons

Courgette is sometimes challenging for younger children as they can find its texture a little 'slimy'. But these batons have a crispy, crunchy texture and a delicious, cheesey flavour.

1 medium courgette
1 egg
1 tbsp milk
60 g (2 oz) dried breadcrumbs
4 tbsp finely grated Parmesan
3 tbsp plain flour
4 tbsp sunflower or canola oil
salt and pepper, to season

* Cut the courgette in half, then into batons roughly 5 cm (2 in) long.
* Beat the egg and milk in a shallow dish with a fork to combine. Put the breadcrumbs in a separate shallow dish and mix in the Parmesan plus salt and pepper to taste.
* Put the flour on a plate and toss the courgette batons in it in batches of 6. Dunk the floured courgette in the egg and milk then toss in the breadcrumbs to coat. Transfer to a plate and repeat with the remaining courgette.
* In a large frying pan, heat 2 tablespoons of the oil over a medium heat and fry half of the bread-crumbed courgette for 3 minutes each side until golden. Drain on kitchen paper and keep warm.
* Wipe out the pan with a piece of kitchen paper and repeat with the remaining oil and courgette. Serve with tomato ketchup.

frittata

This is delicious served hot or cold and it's a good way to use up leftover cooked potato. You can sneak in some hidden veg such as sautéed sweet pepper or courgettes.

4 medium eggs
1 tbsp olive oil
2 medium new potatoes, cooked until tender and diced
1 plum tomato, seeded and diced
2 large spring onions, finely sliced
50 g (2 oz) Cheddar, grated
salt and pepper, to season

* Pre-heat the grill to high. Put the eggs in a jug and beat thoroughly with a fork and season with salt and pepper. In a medium frying pan, heat the oil gently for 1–2 minutes, then add the potatoes, tomato, spring onions and beaten egg. Cook on a low heat for 12–15 minutes until set around the edges but still slightly wobbly in the middle.
* Sprinkle the Cheddar over the top of the frittata and grill for 2–3 minutes until the frittata is set, and the cheese has melted. Slip on to a plate and cut into 4–6 wedges. It is also good served cold cut into squares.

☆ Alternatively, pre-heat the oven to 160°C/300°F/Gas 2. Oil 6 cups of a non-stick muffin pan with the olive oil. Divide the potato, tomato, spring onion and cheese among the muffin cups and then pour on the eggs. Bake for 17–20 minutes until just set in the centre. Run a knife around the edge of the mini frittatas and lift out to serve.

confetti couscous salad

Toast the pine nuts by frying them in a dry frying pan until golden, stirring frequently to make sure that they don't burn.

45 g (1½ oz) couscous
125 ml (4 fl oz) hot vegetable stock
¼ red pepper, diced
¼ orange or yellow pepper, diced
1 small tomato, seeded and chopped
2 spring onions, sliced
1 tbsp raisins
1½ tbsp pine nuts, toasted
salt and pepper, to season

DRESSING

1 tbsp olive oil
1 tsp balsamic vinegar
½ tsp clear honey

* Put the couscous in a bowl. Pour over the hot vegetable stock, cover and leave to stand for 10 minutes, then fluff up with a fork. Stir in the vegetables, raisins and pine nuts.
* Whisk together the ingredients for the dressing and stir into the couscous. Season to taste.

☆ Couscous is grain-like pasta made from wheat and it's popular in Middle Eastern cuisine. You can find it in most supermarkets next to the rice section. What is really good about couscous is the fact that it is really quick and easy to prepare. This could be an option for your child's lunchbox instead of sandwiches. It's also good to keep healthy salads like this in the fridge for your child to snack on during the day.

vegetable quesadillas

A quesadilla (pronounced ke-sah-dee-uh) is a Tex-Mex dish that involves cooking ingredients inside tortillas. I find children like eating tortillas – one of the reasons is that they can eat them with their fingers. You can add other ingredients to this, such as some shredded cooked chicken (see page 128 for Yummy Chicken Quesadillas). To serve, you can use a bought salsa or guacamole or make your own.

½ red pepper, thinly sliced
½ yellow pepper, thinly sliced
1 small red onion, thinly sliced
1 garlic clove, crushed
1 tbsp olive oil
a pinch of cayenne pepper (optional)
2 flour tortillas
85 g (3½ oz) Cheddar, grated
salt and pepper, to season
2 tbsp soured cream, to serve

SALSA
2 medium tomatoes, seeded and diced
1 large spring onion, finely chopped

½ tsp chopped coriander leaves
1 tsp fresh lime juice
a pinch of sugar
salt and pepper, to season

GUACAMOLE
1 large avocado
½ tbsp fresh lemon juice
2 tbsp full-fat soft cheese
1–2 tbsp sliced spring onion
1–2 tbsp diced sweet pepper
salt and pepper, to taste

* Put the peppers, onion, garlic and olive oil in a large non-stick frying pan and stir fry for 6–7 minutes until soft. Season with salt and pepper plus cayenne pepper (if using). Set aside.
* To make the salsa, simply mix together all the ingredients. To make the guacamole, cut the avocado in half, remove the stone and scoop out the flesh. Mash together with the remaining ingredients.
* Wipe out the pan with kitchen paper and lay a tortilla in the base. Spread it with the peppers and onions and sprinkle over the cheese. Place the other tortilla on top and put the pan on a medium heat. Cook for 1½–2 minutes until starting to brown on the base. Flip on to a plate and slide back into the pan to cook the other side for 1½–2 minutes. (If you are worried about flipping the tortillas then grill the top for 1–2 minutes under a hot grill.)
* Slide out of the pan (use a spatula to help) and cut into 6 wedges. Serve with soured cream and salsa (or guacamole).

i don't like...

avacado

(you must be joking)

pancake cannelloni

If your child isn't keen on eating vegetables, try hiding them inside a pancake cannelloni. The recipe given here makes 12–14 pancakes, which is more than you will need for the cannelloni. However, the extra pancakes will keep in the fridge for a couple of days or can be frozen (see My Favourite Pancakes, page 28–9, for storing and reheating instructions).

BATTER

125 g (5 oz) plain flour
1 large egg
300 ml (10 fl oz) milk
1 tbsp butter, melted and cooled, plus extra for frying
a generous pinch of salt

FILLING

200 g (7 oz) fresh spinach or 75 g (2½ oz) frozen spinach
125 g (4½ oz) ricotta
1 × 150 g (5½ oz) ball mozzarella
70 g (2½ oz) freshly grated Parmesan, reserving 2 tbsp for the topping
1 egg yolk, lightly beaten
a pinch of nutmeg (optional)
salt and pepper, to taste

SAUCE

1 × quantity Annabel's Secret Tomato Sauce (page 45)

✳ Put the flour in a large bowl with a pinch of salt. Crack the egg into the middle and add 4 tablespoons of the milk and the melted butter and whisk to make a thick batter. While whisking, gradually pour in the remaining milk. Continue pouring and whisking until you have a batter that is the consistency of slightly thick single cream. Alternatively, you can blitz all the ingredients in a blender. Traditionally, people would say to leave the batter for 30 minutes to allow the starch in the flour to swell, but there's no need to do this. Transfer the batter to a jug.

* Heat a heavy 20-cm (8-in) frying pan over a moderate heat, then grease with a knob of butter. Ladle some batter (approximately 3 tablespoons) into the pan, swirling to coat the base of the pan. Cook for 1–2 minutes until golden at the bottom. Flip over, cook for a further minute, then transfer the pancake to a plate. Repeat until all the batter is used. (If you are making the pancakes in advance, layer them with sheets of greaseproof paper and place in the freezer. To serve, remove from the freezer and defrost, then either microwave for a few seconds or heat in a pan with a little butter.)

* Pre-heat the oven to 200°C/400°F/Gas 6. Prepare the sauce according to the method for Annabel's Secret Tomato Sauce on page 45.

* To make the filling, put the spinach into a large pan, sprinkle with salt and cook for about 3 minutes or until the leaves have wilted. Transfer the spinach to a colander and press out the excess liquid. Place on a chopping board and chop into small pieces.

* In a bowl, mix the chopped spinach with the ricotta, mozzarella, Parmesan, egg yolk and nutmeg, if using. Season with a little salt and pepper.

* Divide the spinach mixture among 8 pancakes (roughly a heaped tablespoon each), spooning into the centre of the pancake and spreading out slightly into a sausage shape. Put one of the pancakes in front of you with the filling facing across. Fold in the left- and right-hand sides of the pancake, so that you have a rectangle shape, and roll up from the short edge closest to you to make a parcel. Put in an oiled baking dish seam-side down and repeat with remaining pancakes.

* Pour the sauce over the pancakes, sprinkle with the remaining mozzarella and Parmesan and bake for 30 minutes or until piping hot. You can also brown the top under the grill if you like.

vegetable kebabs

Children like eating food off a stick or skewer. Here I've marinated some vegetables in balsamic vinegar and honey to give them a delicious flavour. These would be good served with chicken or beef skewers.

¼ yellow pepper
¼ orange or red pepper
1 medium courgette, cut into 1-cm (½-in) thick rounds
MARINADE
2 tbsp olive oil
2 tsp balsamic vinegar
2 tsp clear honey
salt and pepper, to season

∗ Combine the marinade ingredients, then soak the vegetables in this mixture for 1–2 hours.
∗ Pre-heat the grill to high. Thread the vegetables on to four skewers and cook for 2 minutes under the grill. Baste and cook for a further 2 minutes. Turn and baste for 2 minutes then baste and cook for a minute more.

hawaiian chicken salad

Most children love sweet, juicy pineapple and so should be tempted by this salad. It would make a good alternative to sandwiches in your child's lunchbox.

85 g (3 oz) long grain white rice
3 large spring onions, sliced
55 g (2 oz) cooked chicken, cut into small chunks
4 tbsp frozen peas
3 tbsp drained canned sweetcorn
½ × 227 g (8 oz) can pineapple pieces in juice, drained, reserving 2 tbsp juice for the dressing
1 tomato, seeded and diced
DRESSING
2 tbsp canola or sunflower oil
2 tbsp pineapple juice (see above)
1 tsp fresh lemon juice
salt and pepper, to season

∗ Cook the rice according to the packet instructions and leave to cool. Mix together all the ingredients for the chicken salad. Whisk together the dressing ingredients and toss with the salad.

orzo salad

Orzo is tiny pasta that looks like grains of rice. It's popular in the US but you can buy it in the UK in some stores. If you can't find it then use tiny shell-shaped pasta instead (available in my Make Your Own range – see page 224 for details).

55 g (2 oz) orzo
2 tbsp peas, cooked from frozen
4 tbsp drained canned sweetcorn
50 g (2 oz) cooked chicken, cubed

DRESSING

1 tbsp mayonnaise
1 tbsp soured cream or thick Greek yoghurt
1 tsp water
½ tsp white wine vinegar
1½ tsp snipped fresh chives

* Cook the orzo according to the packet instructions. Drain and mix with the peas, sweetcorn and cooked chicken.
* Whisk together all the ingredients for the dressing and toss with the salad.

carrot and cucumber salad

Most kids love cucumber, so here I've combined it with carrot, which is a lot more nutritious as it's a great source of beta-carotene. The Japanese make this salad using seaweed and cucumber, and it's delicious. However, seaweed is pretty hard to find so I have used carrot, cucumber and beansprouts instead.

1 large carrot
½ cucumber
75 g (2½ oz) beansprouts
1 tbsp toasted sesame seeds (optional), for sprinkling

DRESSING

1 tbsp dark soy sauce
1 tbsp rice wine vinegar
1 tbsp sunflower oil
1 tbsp clear honey
1 tsp mirin
1 tsp sesame oil

* Peel the carrot and cucumber, then use a swivel peeler to peel off thin strips.
* Mix together all the ingredients for the dressing, pour over the vegetables and toss. Sprinkle with sesame seeds, if using.

favourite salad dressings

The secret of getting your child to enjoy eating salad is to find a dressing that he or she really likes. I made up a Japanese-style dressing called Dressing For Dinner in my *Favourite Family Recipes* cookbook, which my children absolutely love. I make up six large bottles at a time as they can't get enough of it and use it not only as a dressing but also as a dip for vegetables and as a sauce on foods such as rice or chicken. Try out these tasty dressings and see if you can find one that your child really enjoys.

creamy caesar dressing

This is an easy version of the popular salad dressing.

4 tbsp mayonnaise
2 tbsp freshly grated Parmesan
¼ tsp fresh lemon juice
3 4 drops Worcestershire sauce (or to taste)
4 tbsp cold milk
1 small garlic clove, crushed
salt and freshly ground black pepper, to season

* Whisk together all the ingredients and season to taste with salt and pepper. Store in the fridge for up to 2 weeks and shake well before serving.

tomato balsamic dressing

This is a particular favourite of mine. Use soft sunblush tomatoes, which are sweet, rather than sun-dried tomatoes. If your balsamic vinegar is very sharp, then you may like to add an extra pinch of sugar – it's worth spending a little extra to get a mature balsamic vinegar with a more rounded, sweeter flavour.

2 large ripe tomatoes, roughly chopped
6 tbsp olive oil
3 tbsp balsamic vinegar
2 tsp tomato purée
4 sunblush tomatoes, chopped
1 tbsp sugar (optional)
salt and freshly ground pepper, to season

* Put all of the ingredients into the jug of a blender and whiz for 2 minutes until thoroughly puréed. Season to taste with salt and pepper, then sieve the dressing. Store in a jar in the fridge for up to 2 weeks and shake well before serving.

herby ranch dressing

Traditionally, ranch dressing is made with buttermilk, but I prefer to use thick Greek yoghurt and fresh lemon juice. This also makes a nice dip for vegetable sticks – just reduce the water to 2 tablespoons.

3 tbsp mayonnaise
3 tbsp Greek yoghurt
1 tbsp fresh lemon juice
4 tbsp cold water
½ small garlic clove, crushed (optional)
2 tsp snipped fresh chives
1 tsp chopped fresh parsley
1 tsp chopped fresh coriander, dill
or mint
salt and freshly ground black pepper,
to taste

* Whisk ingredients together. Store in a jar in the fridge for up to 2 weeks and shake well before serving.

oriental salad

I find that children really like the texture of fried rice noodles, so I've combined them with some super-nutritious ingredients such as sunflower and pumpkin seeds, Chinese leaf cabbage and mangetout and tossed everything in a divine dressing. It's so good that I often serve this up to friends who come over to me for supper. Everyone always asks me for the recipe.

sunflower or groundnut oil, for deep frying
50 g (2 oz) fine rice noodles
3 tbsp sunflower seeds
3 tbsp pumpkin seeds
¼ head Chinese leaf cabbage, shredded
2 handfuls of mangetout, cut into matchsticks
2 handfuls of beansprouts

DRESSING
4 tbsp sunflower oil
3 tbsp clear honey
2 tbsp red wine vinegar
1 tbsp dark soy sauce
1 tsp sesame oil
salt and pepper, to season

* Pre-heat the oven to 200°C/400°F/Gas 6. Put 5 cm (2 in) oil in a large deep pan over a medium heat until a cube of bread dropped into the oil turns golden brown in 30 seconds. Separate out the noodles. Drop a small handful of them into the hot oil (be careful as they may spit a bit). The noodles will puff up almost straight away, so remove immediately with a slotted spoon and drain on a tray lined with a double layer of kitchen paper. Allow the oil to reheat for a minute before frying the next batch.
* Spread the seeds on a baking sheet and toast for 8–10 minutes, stirring halfway through. Watch carefully after the first 5 minutes as they can burn easily. Leave to cool.
* Mix the cabbage, mangetout and beansprouts with the noodles and seeds in a big bowl. Whisk the dressing ingredients together with salt and pepper, pour over the salad and toss.

vegetable crisps

I don't normally like beetroot or parsnip, but when they are cooked this way I can't get enough of them. These make a good alternative to a bag of crisps.

225 g (8 oz) mixed root vegetables (e.g. sweet potato, parsnip, carrot, raw beetroot)
sunflower oil, for deep frying
a few cubes of stale bread
freshly ground sea salt and black pepper, to season

* Peel the vegetables and slice them wafer thin using a vegetable peeler or mandoline slicer. Rinse and dry the slices.
* Put enough oil in a deep-fat fryer or large pan to come about one-third to halfway up the pan. Heat the oil and test whether it is hot enough by tossing a bread cube into the pan. If it turns golden within about 30 seconds, the oil is ready. Add the vegetables separately and fry in batches. They will turn golden within a few minutes. Remove them straight away using the basket of the deep-fat fryer or a slotted spoon and drain on kitchen paper. Sprinkle with salt and pepper. Allow to cool and then store in an airtight container.

☆ You can also cook the crisps in the oven. Simply toss in a large bowl with some oil and seasoning, spread out on a non-stick baking sheet and bake at 200°C/400°F/Gas 6 for 12–15 minutes or until golden, turning halfway through.

spicy potato wedges

If your child likes chips, you might want to opt for a healthier version that is baked in the oven rather than fried. These are particularly good when dipped in soured cream or the Herby Ranch Dressing (page 58).

2 medium white potatoes (Desirée or Yukon)
2 tbsp sunflower or canola oil
1–2 tsp Fajita spice mix
salt, to season

* Pre-heat oven to 200°C/400°F/Gas 6.
* Cut the potatoes in half then each half into 6 wedges. Put in a colander and rinse well with cold water. Pat dry thoroughly with a clean tea towel or kitchen paper.
* Put the oil and spice mix in a large bowl and mix. Toss the wedges in the oil and lay out on a large baking sheet (you can line the baking sheet with foil for an easy clean-up). Bake for 30 minutes, turning halfway. Allow to cool for 5 minutes then sprinkle with a little salt before serving.

☆ Mix a little salt and pepper with paprika, garlic powder or rosemary as an alternative flavouring for the wedges.

root vegetable chips

Another delicious alternative to ordinary chips. This might be a good way to encourage your child to try other vegetables. You could brush the vegetables with a little clear honey for the last 5–10 minutes (not earlier or they will burn), and you could season with a little ground coriander if your child likes this.

1 medium parsnip
1 small sweet potato
1 large carrot
2 tbsp sunflower oil or canola oil
salt, to season

* Pre-heat oven to 200°C/400°F/Gas 6.
* Peel the vegetables and cut into sticks roughly 6–7 cm (2–3 in) long and 1 cm (½ in) thick. Put in a large bowl with the oil and toss to coat thoroughly.
* Spread out on a large baking sheet (lined with foil if you want to make the clean-up easier) and bake for 30 minutes, turning halfway through. Allow to cool for 5 minutes, then sprinkle with a little salt before serving.

mini sweetcorn fritters

My daughter Lara really likes these. She often has them as a snack so I keep a supply of them in the freezer. To freeze them, wrap the cooled fritters in foil in a single layer with 2 fritters per packet. To serve, pre-heat the oven to 180°C/350°F/Gas 4 and put the frozen fritters on a baking sheet. Bake for approximately 8 minutes until hot. These fritters can also be made with gluten-free flour.

30 g (1 oz) plain flour
½ tsp baking powder
¼ tsp salt
1 large egg
1 × 200 g can sweetcorn, drained
1 large or 2 small spring onions, finely sliced
2 tbsp sunflower or canola oil, for frying

* Whiz together all the ingredients except the oil in the bowl of a food processor for 1 minute to make a batter.
* Heat a little of the oil in a large frying pan and drop in tablespoonfuls of the batter. Cook for 1–1½ minutes in two batches of 5 until golden on the underside, then carefully turn and cook for a further minute. You can use the back of a spoon to help push the fritter on to a spatula to make turning easier. Drain briefly on kitchen paper before serving.

mini sweetcorn fritters

TIP:
Experts recommend that we should eat 5 daily servings of fruit and vegetables. Three tablespoons of sweetcorn counts as one serving of fruit and vegetables.

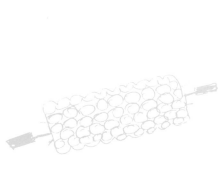

funky fish

how to get your child to eat fish

* There's nothing worse than dry overcooked fish. Raw fish is slightly translucent. As soon as it becomes opaque all the way through, it is cooked.

* Always check carefully for bones. Even filleted fish can have small bones and this could put your child off eating fish.

* There are lots of tasty ways to coat fish: try using crushed cornflakes, popcorn and grated cheese, or even crushed cream crackers.

* Children like to eat with their fingers so give recipes like marinated salmon on a skewer, mini fishcakes or prawn toast.

* Sardines mashed with a little tomato ketchup or tuna mixed with sweetcorn, spring onion and mayonnaise make good sandwich fillings.

* Make individual fish pies in mini ramekins. It looks much more appealing than a dollop of fish pie on a plate and you can make a few at a time and pop some in the freezer.

* Children can be fascinated by the different kinds of fish in a fish shop. You might like to take them with you occasionally and see if they can name the different types of fish.

super salmon wrap

Unlike canned tuna, a can of salmon still contains some omega-3 brain-boosting fatty acids.

1 tbsp mayonnaise
1½ tsp chilli ketchup or 1½ tbsp tomato ketchup plus a few drops of Tabasco sauce
½ tsp fresh lemon juice
2 tbsp canned red salmon, flaked
½ tomato, seeded and diced
1-cm (½-in) thick chunk cucumber, diced
1 small spring onion, finely sliced
1 flour tortilla

* Mix together the mayonnaise, ketchup and lemon juice. Stir in the flaked salmon, tomato, cucumber and spring onion.
* Heat the tortilla for a few seconds in a microwave or dry frying pan. Arrange the filling near one end of the tortilla and roll up. Cut the tortilla in half diagonally and serve.

annabel's tasty prawn wrap

Wraps are the new, trendy sandwich, and prawns in cocktail sauce are generally popular with children, so this makes a good combination. As you can see, it's very easy to make your own cocktail sauce. This would also make a good sandwich filling.

2 tbsp mayonnaise
1 tsp tomato ketchup
½ tsp fresh lemon juice
2–3 drops Worcestershire sauce
40 g (1½ oz) cooked prawns
½ medium tomato, seeded and diced
1 small spring onion, thinly sliced
1 wheat tortilla
a handful of shredded lettuce (Little Gem or iceberg)

* Mix together the mayonnaise, ketchup, lemon juice and Worcestershire sauce. Stir in the prawns, tomato and spring onion.
* Heat the tortilla for 20 seconds on full power in a microwave or for about 15 seconds in a dry frying pan. Arrange the prawn mixture near one end of the tortilla, cover with shredded lettuce and roll up. Cut the tortilla in half diagonally and serve.

prawn toasts

TIP:
When I take my children to a Chinese restaurant they love the food so it's a good idea to make your own Chinese food at home and get your children to help in the kitchen.

prawn toasts

Ever noticed how much kids eat when you take them out for a Chinese meal? So why don't they eat like that at home?! Prawn toasts are always popular and there's usually a fight over who is going to eat the last one. So maybe here's a way to get your kids to appreciate your home cooking.

110 g (4 oz) cooked peeled prawns
1 medium egg white
1 large spring onion, finely sliced
2 slices white bread, crusts removed
1 tbsp sesame seeds
4 tbsp sunflower oil or canola oil, for frying
a large pinch of salt

* Put the prawns, egg white and onion into a food processor with a large pinch of salt and whiz to a paste. Spread the mixture over the 2 slices of bread. Sprinkle over the sesame seeds and cut each slice into 4 squares or triangles.
* Put 3 tablespoons of the oil in a large non-stick frying pan over a medium heat for 2–3 minutes. Fry the prawn toasts bread-side down for 2½–3 minutes until golden on the underside. Reduce the heat slightly. Turn the toasts, add the remaining tablespoon of oil and fry for a further 2–3 minutes until golden. Transfer the cooked toasts (bread side down) to a double layer of kitchen towel and allow to cool for a couple of minutes before serving.

salmon on a stick with stir-fried noodles

These salmon 'lollipops' with a slightly sweet glaze are a good way to tempt children who may shy away from fish.

2 tbsp fresh orange juice
1½ tbsp clear honey
2 tsp dark soy sauce
150 g (5½ oz) skinless salmon fillet (needs to be 2 cm/1 in thick, so not tail end)

NOODLES
70 g (2½ oz) medium egg noodles, cooked according to the packet instructions or ready-to-use fine thread noodles
½ tsp sesame oil
1 tsp sunflower oil
a handful of mangetout, cut into matchsticks
¼ red or orange pepper, cut into thin strips
2 spring onions, sliced
a handful of beansprouts
1 tbsp dark soy sauce
1 tbsp sesame seeds, lightly toasted

∗ You will also need 2 bamboo skewers that have been soaked in water.
∗ Put the orange juice, honey and soy sauce in a small pan. Bring to the boil and cook for about a minute or until thickened slightly. Allow to cool.
∗ Pre-heat the grill to high. Meanwhile, cut the salmon in half lengthways and thread on to two skewers. Fold any thin belly pieces over so that the fish is even thickness. Put on a foil-lined grill tray. Brush on some sauce and grill for 2 minutes. Brush again and grill for 1 minute. Turn the salmon over, and repeat.
∗ If the salmon is particularly thick, baste the sides with the juices from the pan and grill for 1 minute each side (as close to the grill as possible). Reserve leftover sauce for the noodles. Keep the salmon warm while you cook the noodles.
∗ Cook the noodles according to the packet instructions and drain (or use ready-cooked noodles). Toss them in the sesame oil. Heat the sunflower oil in a wok and stir fry the mangetout, pepper and spring onions for 2–3 minutes. Add the beansprouts and noodles and cook for 1½–2 minutes. Toss in the leftover salmon cooking sauce with 2 tablespoons water, soy sauce and sesame seeds.

tuna melt fishcakes

Adding ketchup to a recipe gives it a little more child appeal.
For a gluten-free option, use polenta instead of breadcrumbs
and gluten-free flour for dusting.

350 g (12 oz) potatoes
2 tbsp mayonnaise
2 tbsp tomato ketchup
2 × 200 g can tuna in water, drained and flaked
4 spring onions, finely chopped
1 tsp fresh lemon juice
3 tbsp plain flour, seasoned with salt and pepper
1 egg, beaten with 1 tbsp milk
70 g (2½ oz) breadcrumbs
85 g (3 oz) Cheddar, grated
salt and pepper, to season

* Pre-heat the oven to 200°C/400°F/Gas 6.
* Peel and boil the potatoes and mash with the mayonnaise and ketchup. Stir in
the tuna, spring onions and lemon juice. Form into 8 fishcakes. Dust the cakes
with the flour, dip in the beaten egg and milk and coat in the breadcrumbs.
* Put the fishcakes on an oiled baking sheet and bake in the oven for 10 minutes.
Turn over and bake for a further 5 minutes, then sprinkle the grated Cheddar on
top and bake for 5 minutes more. (You can brown under a hot grill for a couple
of minutes after baking, if you like.)

salmon fishcakes

There are two versions of these salmon fishcakes. You can make them without a breadcrumb coating (as here), or if you want them as child-friendly finger food, roll the mixture into 12 balls, dust in flour, dip in beaten egg then coat in breadcrumbs. You will need about 45 g (1½ oz) fresh white breadcrumbs. You can then either shallow fry or cook in a deep fryer.

1 medium potato
70 g (2½ oz) salmon
a squeeze of lemon juice (for microwave method)
a knob of butter (for microwave method)
150 ml (5 fl oz) fish stock (for poaching)
2 spring onions, chopped
1 tsp sweet chilli sauce
2 tbsp tomato ketchup
½ tbsp mayonnaise
salt and pepper, to taste
1 tbsp seasoned flour, for dusting
2 tbsp sunflower oil, for frying

* Boil the unpeeled potato in salted water for 25–30 minutes until tender (to a table knife). Drain and, when cool enough to handle, peel and mash. Cook the salmon in the microwave for a couple of minutes with the lemon juice and butter. Alternatively poach for c ouple of minutes in the fish stock. Strain if poaching, and flake on to a plate. Leave to cool slightly.
* Mix the potato with the spring onions, chilli sauce, ketchup, mayonnaise and salt and pepper to taste. Fold in the flaked salmon, being careful not to break up the fish too much. Take tablespoonfuls of the mixture and form into small cakes. Dust in seasoned flour.
* Heat the oil in a non-stick pan and fry the fishcakes for 2–3 minutes each side until golden.

salmon and cod in a chive sauce

That old saying 'fish is good for the brain' is absolutely true. Oil-rich fish such as salmon, fresh tuna and sardines are a rich source of brain-boosting omega-3 fatty acids, which are vital for brain function and can help the performance of dyslexic, hyperactive children.

25 g (1 oz) shallots, diced
15 g (½ oz) butter
2 tbsp white wine vinegar
15 g (½ oz) plain flour
250 ml (9 fl oz) fish stock (you could use a fish-stock cube)
40 g (1½ oz) frozen peas
3 tbsp single cream
½ tsp fresh lemon juice
2 tsp finely snipped fresh chives
125 g (4½ oz) each salmon and cod fillet, skinned and cut
into 2½ cm (1 in) cubes

* Sweat the shallots in the butter for about 5 minutes until soft but not coloured. Add the vinegar and boil until just evaporated. Stir in the flour and cook gently for 2 minutes, stirring occasionally.
* Whisk in the stock. Bring to the boil, stirring, and boil until reduced by half. Add the peas halfway through. Remove from the heat and stir in the cream, a squeeze of lemon and the chives.
* Put the fish in a suitable microwave dish together with the peas. Pour over the sauce. Cover with cling film, prick the top and cook in the microwave (900-w full power) for about 2½ minutes. Alternatively, add the fish to the saucepan with the peas and poach in the sauce for about 4 minutes or until cooked through. Serve with fluffy white rice if liked.

fabulous fish pie

450 g (1 lb) potatoes, peeled and cut into chunks
200 g (7 oz) carrots, peeled and sliced
3 tbsp milk
50 g (2 oz) butter
300 g (11 oz) baby spinach, carefully washed
250 g (9 oz) salmon fillet, skinned and cut into 2-cm (1-in) cubes
250 g (9 oz) cod fillet, skinned and cut into 2 cm (1-in) cubes
1 egg, lightly beaten
salt and white pepper, to season

WHITE SAUCE

25 g (1 oz) butter
1 small onion, peeled and chopped
25 g (1 oz) flour
150 ml (5 fl oz) milk
100 ml (3½ fl oz) vegetable or chicken stock
¼ tsp Dijon mustard
1 tbsp finely chopped parsley
1 bay leaf
50 g (2 oz) mature Cheddar, grated
salt and pepper, to season

* Pre-heat the oven to 180°C/350°F/Gas 4. Bring a pan of lightly salted water to the boil, add the potatoes, reduce the heat and cook for 15 minutes. Steam the carrots for about 20 minutes or until tender. Return the vegetables to the pan and mash with the milk and half the butter until smooth. Season to taste.
* Wash the spinach and add to a hot pan for a few minutes until wilted. Drain and gently squeeze out the excess water. Melt the remaining butter in a pan, sauté the spinach for a couple of minutes and season.
* To make the white sauce, melt the butter and sauté the onion until softened. Add the flour and cook for about 30 seconds, stirring occasionally. Gradually stir in the milk, vegetable stock and mustard. Bring to the boil and cook for a couple of minutes. Add the fish with the parsley and bay leaf and simmer for 4–5 minutes. Remove the bay leaf and stir in the cheese until melted. Season well.
* Put the fish in the sauce into a 18-cm (7-in) round ovenproof dish. Arrange the spinach on top then cover with the mashed potato and carrot. Make a design with a fork and brush with the beaten egg. Bake for 30–35 minutes.

mini fish pies

I design the menus for one of the largest chains of nurseries in the UK and one of the children's favourite dishes is this fish pie. Another of their favourite recipes is my fruity curried chicken, so it's interesting to see that children often have more sophisticated taste than we imagine. Making food look attractive is important and so it seems much more appealing to make individual fish pies rather than have a dollop of food on the plate.

POTATO TOPPING
800 g (1¾ lb) potatoes
30 g (1 oz) butter
7 tbsp milk
4 tbsp freshly grated Parmesan
1 egg, lightly beaten
salt and freshly ground black pepper, to taste

SAUCE
45 g (1½ oz) butter
1 large shallot, diced
2 tbsp white wine vinegar
45 g (1½ oz) flour
450 ml (16 fl oz) fish stock
6 tbsp double cream
1½ tsp chopped fresh dill or snipped fresh chives
salt and freshly ground black pepper, to season

SALMON AND COD FILLING
250 g (9 oz) salmon, skin removed and cut into 2-cm (¾-in) chunks
250 g (9 oz) cod, skin removed and cut into 2-cm (¾-in) chunks
150 g (5½ oz) small cooked prawns
70 g (2½ oz) frozen peas

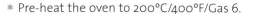

* Pre-heat the oven to 200°C/400°F/Gas 6.
* Boil the potatoes in salted water. Drain and mash with the butter, milk and Parmesan and season to taste.
* To make the sauce, melt the butter and sauté the shallot for 5–6 minutes until soft. Add the white wine vinegar and boil for 2–3 minutes until the liquid has evaporated. Stir in the flour to make a roux. Gradually, stir in the fish stock and then cook over a medium heat, stirring continuously. Bring to the boil then cook, stirring, until thickened. Remove from the heat and stir in the cream and the chopped dill or chives. Season well as the fish is unseasoned.
* Divide all the fish and peas among four or six mini ramekins (depending on the size) and pour over the sauce. If you have time, allow the fish, pea and sauce filling to cool and become less liquid and easier to cover with the mashed potato without it sinking into the filling. Brush the potato topping with a little beaten egg. Bake for 25 minutes.

sizzling asian shrimp

A lot of my more popular recipes for children are Asian-style dishes. It's also good to flavour thin fillets of white fish with garlic, ginger, spring onion and soy sauce and cook them wrapped in foil.

2 tsp sunflower oil
1 tsp grated fresh ginger
1 garlic clove, crushed
340 g (12 oz) shelled raw tiger prawns (defrosted frozen prawns are fine)
2 tsp sesame oil
2 large or 4 small spring onions, thinly sliced
1 tbsp fresh lime juice
a handful fresh coriander leaves, to serve (optional)

* Heat the sunflower oil in a wok until sizzling. Add the ginger, garlic and prawns and cook for 1–1½ minutes, then turn the prawns and cook for another 1–2 minutes until the prawns have turned pink. Add the sesame oil, spring onions and the lime juice and stir for 30 seconds until fragrant.
* Remove from the heat and serve with the coriander leaves scattered over.

golden fish fingers

Crushed cornflakes make a delicious coating. If you like, you could add a pinch of cayenne pepper. Serve with home-made tartare sauce or just tomato ketchup.

30 g (1 oz) cornflakes
200 g (7 oz) cod fillets, skinned (or use plaice or sole)
20 g (¾ oz) plain flour, for coating
1 egg, lightly beaten
1½ tbsp sunflower oil
salt and pepper, to season
TARTARE SAUCE
150 ml (5 fl oz) mayonnaise
fresh lemon juice, to taste
1 tbsp chopped parsley
1 tbsp capers, chopped
2 tsp chopped gherkins
1 tbsp snipped chives

* Put the cornflakes in a plastic bag, crush using a rolling pin and spread out on a plate. Cut the fish into 6 strips and season with salt and pepper. Coat with flour. Dip into lightly beaten egg then coat with the crushed cornflakes.
* Heat the oil in a frying pan and sauté the fish for 3–4 minutes or until golden and cooked through, turning halfway through.
* To make the tartare sauce, simply mix together all the sauce ingredients. Serve with the fish fingers.

crunchy popcorn fish

You don't always have to coat fish in breadcrumbs. Why not try and entice kids to eat more fish by coating it with popcorn or crisps? If using crisps, I would use half a large packet. If using plain crisps, add 30 g (1 oz) freshly grated Parmesan and some paprika or use flavoured crisps. You can use gluten-free flour instead of plain flour. You could serve these with tomato ketchup or tartare sauce (see Golden Fish Fingers, page 81).

40 g (1½ oz) lightly salted popcorn
40 g (1½ oz) mature Cheddar, grated
30 g (1 oz) fresh grated Parmesan
1 tsp paprika
4 × 150 g (5½ oz) skinless cod or salmon fillets
2 tbsp plain flour
2 eggs, beaten with a pinch of salt
2–3 tbsp sunflower oil, for frying
salt and pepper, to season

* Put popcorn, cheeses and paprika in a food processor and whiz for 1–2 minutes until the popcorn is reduced to crumbs. Season to taste with plenty of pepper, then spread out on a large plate.
* Cut the fish into strips about the size of a fish finger, season with a little salt, dust with flour, dip in the beaten egg and coat in the popcorn mixture.
* Heat the oil in a large frying pan and cook the fish over a medium heat for 2–3 minutes on each side, until the coating is crispy and the fish is just cooked. Drain briefly on kitchen towel before serving.

bag-baked cod niçoise

The flavours of the South of France in individual parcels. Baking fish in a parcel keeps it wonderfully moist and seals in the flavour. You might think it strange that I am using olives – my daughter liked eating olives at the age of two and, surprisingly, they are popular with quite a few children. If your child doesn't like olives you could use four chopped sunblush tomatoes instead.

1 small red onion, diced
1 tsp olive oil
1 small garlic clove, crushed
1 tsp balsamic vinegar
½ tsp sugar
225 g (8 oz) cherry tomatoes, quartered
6–7 stoned black olives, quartered
4 skinless cod fillets, about 150 g (5½ oz) each
salt and pepper, to taste
12 basil leaves, to serve (optional)

* You will also need 4 large squares of foil for the parcels.
* Sauté the onion in the oil for 7–8 minutes until soft. Add the garlic and balsamic vinegar and cook until the vinegar has evaporated, then stir in the sugar, tomatoes and olives and cook for 2–3 minutes, until the tomatoes start to soften. Remove from the heat and season to taste with salt and pepper. Allow to cool slightly (you can make this in advance and store in the fridge for up to 2 days).
* Pre-heat the oven to 200°C/400°F/Gas 6. Lay a piece of fish in the centre of each foil square and season with salt and pepper. Put a quarter of the tomato mixture on top of each piece of fish, then bring the edges of each square of foil together and scrunch to seal. Put the 4 parcels on a baking sheet and bake for 8 minutes until the cod is opaque and starting to flake. Thick pieces of fish may take 2–3 minutes longer.
* Serve the fish with the tomato mixture and any juices from the parcel spooned over the top and garnished with basil leaves.

PREPARATION TIME 10 MINUTES
COOKING TIME 10 MINUTES
MAKES 2 PORTIONS
SUITABLE FOR FREEZING

sweet-and-sour fish

If you are having difficulty getting your child to eat fish, you might like to try making this sweet and sour sauce. The sauce will mask any strong fishy taste. This would also work using chicken breasts cut into cubes and chicken stock instead of fish stock.

200 g (7 oz) cod fillets, skinned and cut into cubes, or sole fillets, skinned and cut into strips
plain flour, seasoned with salt and pepper
1½ tbsp vegetable oil

SWEET AND SOUR SAUCE
100 ml (3½ fl oz) fish stock (use half a cube)
1 tbsp white wine vinegar
1 tbsp caster sugar
1½ tbsp tomato ketchup
½ tbsp soy sauce
½ tbsp cornflour
3 tbsp water
½ tsp sesame oil
1 tbsp finely sliced spring onion

∗ Coat the fish in the seasoned flour. Heat the vegetable oil in a frying pan and sauté for 3–4 minutes or until cooked (it should flake easily with a fork).
∗ Mix the ingredients for the sauce and heat gently in a pan, stirring until thickened. Pour the sauce over the fish, heat through and serve on a bed of fluffy white rice if liked.

drunken fish with little trees

The secret to getting fussy eaters to enjoy eating fish is to come up with a tasty sauce. This Chinese-style sauce is popular with my three children and it takes only a few minutes to prepare. Giving food fun names can encourage children to eat – for instance, 'little trees' is a good way to describe broccoli florets. Interestingly, many children who are not keen on other green vegetables do enjoy broccoli.

100 g (3½ oz) broccoli florets
350 g (12 oz) plaice fillets, cut into 6-cm (2-in) strips, or cod fillets
cut into 4-cm (1½-in) cubes
30 g (1 oz) plain flour, seasoned with salt and pepper
1½ tbsp sunflower oil

CHINESE-STYLE SAUCE
250 ml (9 fl oz) chicken stock
2 tsp dark soy sauce
1 tsp sesame oil
1 tbsp caster sugar
1 tsp cider vinegar
1 tbsp cornflour
1 spring onion, finely sliced

* To make the sauce, mix together the stock, soy sauce, sesame oil, sugar, vinegar and cornflour. Pour the mixture into a saucepan. Bring to the boil then simmer for 2–3 minutes until thickened and smooth. Stir in the spring onion.
* Steam the broccoli florets for about 5 minutes or until just tender. Meanwhile, toss the fish in the seasoned flour to coat. Heat the sunflower oil in a frying pan and sauté the fish for a couple of minutes each side until just cooked.
* Pour the sauce over the fish, add the broccoli florets and heat through for about a minute before serving.

pork and peanut noodles

If you have a fussy eater who likes peanut butter, try this recipe. To make life easier, you can buy pre-cooked straight-to-wok rice noodles in packets in some supermarkets, which are really very good.

150 g (5½ oz) thin rice noodles or pre-cooked straight-to-wok noodles
1 tbsp sunflower oil
1 small onion, peeled and sliced
1 garlic clove, crushed
250 g (9 oz) minced pork or chicken
100 g (3½ oz) small mangetout, sliced in half
2 tbsp crunchy peanut butter
2 tsp soft light brown sugar
1 tbsp dark soy sauce
100 ml (3½ fl oz) chicken stock
1 tsp finely chopped red chilli, seeded
a small bunch of fresh coriander, chopped (optional)

* Place the noodles in a bowl, cover with boiling water and leave to soak for 5 minutes, then drain. Alternatively, you can use a packet of pre-cooked straight-to-wok rice noodles.
* Heat the oil in a wok or frying pan, then sauté the onion for 4 minutes. Add the garlic and cook for 1 minute. Add the pork or chicken mince and stir fry for about 8 minutes or until the juices have evaporated and the meat is starting to look crisp. Throw in the mangetout and cook for 2 minutes.
* Meanwhile mix together the peanut butter, brown sugar, soy sauce, stock and chilli. Add the peanut sauce and the noodles to the wok or frying pan, toss well and stir fry for about 1 minute or until heated through. Before serving, you could sprinkle with a little coriander.

hidden vegetable spaghetti bolognese

This Bolognese sauce sneaks in five vegetables, and it tastes great even to confirmed veggie haters – what you can't see you can't complain about! You can also use this sauce to make shepherd's pie or lasagne (see pages 139 and 96).

2 tbsp olive oil
75 g (2¾ oz) red onion, finely chopped
55 g (2 oz) leek, finely sliced
60 g (2 oz) mushrooms, sliced
85 g (3½ oz) carrot, grated
3 g (1 oz) celery, diced
1 garlic clove, crushed
150 ml (5 fl oz) beef stock
250 g (9 oz) minced beef
2 × 400 g cans chopped tomatoes
3 tbsp tomato purée
1 tbsp sun-dried tomato paste
1 tsp caster sugar
300 g (10½ oz) spaghetti

* Heat 1 tablespoon of the oil and sauté the onion for 3 minutes. Add the remaining vegetables and sauté for 7 minutes. Add the garlic and sauté for 1 minute. Add the stock and simmer for 10 minutes, then blitz in a food processor.
* Heat the remaining tablespoon of oil in a large frying pan and brown the mince for 5 minutes, breaking up well with a fork or wooden spoon. Add the chopped tomatoes, tomato purée, sun-dried tomato paste and sugar and cook for 30 minutes. Add the vegetable purée and continue to cook for 2 minutes more.
* Meanwhile, cook the spaghetti according to the packet instructions. Drain and toss with the sauce.

mummy's pot noodles

Always popular with kids, but the ones you buy are really high in salt. It only takes a few minutes to make your own! It's fun to serve them in a cup, a bit like pot noodles.

70 g (2½ oz) fine Chinese-style dried egg noodles or use straight-to-wok fine thread noodles
125 ml (4 fl oz) chicken stock
1½ tsp dark soy sauce
25 g (1 oz) frozen peas
35 g (1½ oz) drained canned or frozen sweetcorn
50 g (2 oz) cooked chicken, shredded
½ tsp cornflour

* Cook the noodles according to the packet instructions (or use pre-cooked noodles). Drain and set aside. Put the stock, soy sauce, peas, sweetcorn and chicken in a pan over a medium heat. Bring to a simmer and cook for 2 minutes.
* In a small cup, mix the cornflour with 1 teaspoon of cold water and add to the contents of the pan then cook, stirring, for a further minute until the liquid thickens slightly. Add the noodles and reheat briefly, stirring. Transfer to a bowl to serve.

pasta with tomato and mascarpone sauce

My children, like most, prefer pasta with tomato sauce, so I always try to add other ingredients such as chopped vegetables, which I purée into the sauce. It's nice to make a slightly creamy tomato sauce by stirring in some mascarpone cheese. The novelty-shaped pasta adds child interest. This sauce would also be good with steamed white fish or poached chicken.

1 tbsp olive oil
1 red onion, peeled and chopped
30 g (1 oz) carrot
30 g (1 oz) courgette
15 g (½ oz) celery
1 garlic clove, crushed
50 g (2 oz) button mushrooms
400 g (14 oz) passata
½ tsp sugar
2 tbsp torn basil leaves (optional)
100 g (3½ oz) mascarpone cheese
200 g (7 oz) animal or alphabet-shaped pasta (or any novelty shape)
salt and freshly ground black pepper (for babies over 1 year), to season

* Heat the oil in a saucepan and sauté the onion, carrot, courgette and celery for 5 minutes. Add the garlic and sauté for 1 minute. Add the mushrooms and sauté for 2 minutes. Stir in the passata and sugar, and simmer for 10 minutes with the lid on, stirring occasionally.
* Remove from the heat, add the basil and blend in a food processor. Return to the pan and add the mascarpone cheese. Stir until melted and simmer for 1–2 minutes. Season to taste.
* In the meantime, cook the pasta according to the packet instructions in a large pan of salted boiling water. Drain and toss with the sauce.

nicholas's lasagne

My son Nicholas started out as a fussy eater but now eats
absolutely anything. I think he really appreciates home cooking
since he has been at university. He comes home most weekends
to eat, calling me from the station to ensure that the food will
be on the table when he walks in the door! This lasagne is one
of his favourites.

9 no-cook dried lasagne sheets
75 g (2½ oz) Cheddar, grated
30 g (1 oz) freshly grated Parmesan
BOLOGNESE SAUCE
1 quantity Hidden Vegetable Bolognese Sauce (page 91)
BÉCHAMEL SAUCE
55 g (2 oz) butter
55 g (2 oz) plain flour
600 ml (20 fl oz) milk
a pinch of grated nutmeg
¼ tsp Dijon mustard

* Prepare the Bolognese sauce, according to instructions on page 91.
* Pre-heat the oven to 200°C/400°F/Gas 6. Make a Béchamel sauce by melting
the butter, then stirring in the flour. Cook for 1 minute, then stir in the milk a
little at a time. Bring to a simmer, stirring constantly, and season the sauce
well with salt and pepper, a good pinch of nutmeg and the mustard.
* Spread a quarter of the Béchamel in a thin layer in the bottom of an
ovenproof dish (18 cm × 29 cm/7 in × 12 in) and add a layer of pasta on top
(three lasagne sheets). Spoon on another quarter of the Béchamel and spread
over the pasta, then top with half of the Bolognese. Repeat the pasta, Béchamel,
Bolognese then a top layer of pasta and spoon over the remaining Béchamel.
Scatter on the cheeses and bake for 40 minutes, until piping hot. Allow to
stand for 10 minutes before serving.

PREPARATION TIME 8 MINUTES
COOKING TIME 12 MINUTES
MAKES 4 PORTIONS
SUITABLE FOR FREEZING

marina's pasta with pesto and cherry tomatoes

Marina is from the Philippines and has been helping me in the kitchen for more than 15 years. Not only is she a fabulous cook but she is also a dear friend and we often spend time testing and inventing recipes together.

250 g (9 oz) fusilli
2 tbsp light olive oil
100 g (4 oz) onion, sliced
1 garlic clove, crushed
200 g (7 oz) chicken breast, cut into strips
200 g (7 oz) cherry tomatoes, halved
3 tbsp green pesto
1 tbsp dark soy sauce
1 tbsp balsamic vinegar
salt and freshly ground black pepper, to season
freshly grated Parmesan, to serve (optional)

* Cook the fusilli in lightly salted boiling water according to the packet instructions. Drain and set aside.
* Heat the oil in a large frying pan or wok. Sauté the onion for 3 minutes, stirring occasionally, then add the garlic and cook for 1 minute. Add the chicken and stir fry for 2 minutes, then add the tomatoes and fry for a further 2 minutes until the chicken is cooked through and the tomatoes are soft. Add the pesto, soy sauce and balsamic vinegar and cook for 1 minute. Add the pasta and season to taste with a little salt and pepper and continue to cook for a minute or so until heated through. If you like, you can sprinkle with Parmesan before serving.

☆ I find that quite a few children really like pesto. There is a selection of really good ready-made pestos available in the supermarket so try adding some to your child's pasta together with fresh ingredients.

fresh tomato sauce for spaghetti

This is one of my children's favourite meals. You will need to choose good-quality, ripe plum tomatoes to get the best flavour – look for ones with a dark-red colour. Tomatoes are a good source of lycopene, a powerful antioxidant that helps prevent heart disease and cancer. Interestingly, they are better for you cooked in a little oil or butter, as this helps our bodies to absorb the lycopene more efficiently.

2 tbsp olive oil
2 small onions, chopped
1 fat garlic clove, crushed
10 large plum tomatoes, skinned, seeded and diced
1 tsp sugar
25 g (1 oz) butter
8 fresh basil leaves, torn into pieces
250g (9 oz) spaghetti
salt and freshly ground black pepper, to taste
freshly grated Parmesan, to serve (optional)

* Heat the oil and sauté the onion and garlic for 3 minutes. Skin the whole tomatoes by scoring a cross in the bottom of each and placing about four at a time in a large pan of boiling water for about 15 seconds. Using a slotted spoon, transfer the tomatoes into a bowl of iced water. When cool enough to handle, remove from the water and pull off the skins using your fingers or a small knife. Seeded tomatoes make thicker sauces – it's easy to remove the seeds using a melon baller or teaspoon.
* Dice the tomatoes and add with the sugar to the onions. Cook for 30 minutes. Stir in the butter and basil leaves and season to taste. Some children are put off if they see green bits in their tomato sauce so you may want to divide the sauce into two and add basil to only one half – offer the sauce with the basil first.
* In the meantime, cook the spaghetti according to the packet instructions in a large pan of salted boiling water. Drain and toss with the sauce. If you like, sprinkle over the Parmesan to serve.

i don't like...

anything with basil

mighty mac and cheese

I know lots of fussy children who only ever want to eat plain pasta with grated cheese. Maybe with a little gentle persuasion they could be enticed to try this tasty macaroni cheese. You can make it with or without the ham and tomato – it's a really delicious cheese sauce. Pasta provides a good source of complex carbohydrate, so this macaroni will boost your child's energy levels as well as providing a good source of protein and calcium.

350 g (12 oz) macaroni
4 medium tomatoes, skinned, seeded and chopped
75 g (2½ oz) sliced ham, shredded (optional)

CHEESE SAUCE
45 g (1½ oz) butter
45 g (1½ oz) flour
450 ml (16 fl oz) milk
85 g (3 oz) Gruyère, grated
60 g (2 oz) freshly grated Parmesan
150 g (5½ oz) mascarpone cheese

TOPPING
40 g (1½ oz) breadcrumbs (2 medium slices bread,
white or wholemeal, crusts removed)
20 g (¾ oz) freshly grated Parmesan

* Cook the pasta according the packet instructions in plenty of salted boiling water.
* Melt the butter, stir in the flour and cook for 1 minute. Gradually add the milk, stirring over a low heat for 5–6 minutes. Take off the heat, stir in the Gruyère and Parmesan until melted, then the mascarpone cheese.
* Drain the pasta, return to the pan, pour over the cheese sauce and heat through gently. Stir in the chopped tomatoes and shredded ham.
* Transfer to a greased ovenproof dish (approximately 26 cm × 17 cm × 5 cm/ 9 in × 6 in × 2 in). Mix together the breadcrumbs and Parmesan and sprinkle on top. Place under a preheated grill until golden and bubbling.

animal pasta salad with multicoloured veggies

This can be served warm or cold. It's a good idea to keep a bowl of it in the fridge for your child to snack on during the day. It would also be good as a change from sandwiches in your child's lunchbox. You can omit the chicken for vegetarians.

150 g (5½ oz) Animal Pasta shapes
1 medium carrot, peeled and cut into matchsticks
50 g (2 oz) each broccoli and cauliflower, cut into small florets
50 g (2 oz) French beans, topped and tailed and cut in half
½ sweet red pepper, diced
1 medium/large courgette, trimmed and cut into matchsticks
100 g (3½ oz) drained canned sweetcorn
75 g (2½ oz) cooked chicken, diced (optional)
DRESSING
2 tbsp cider or red wine vinegar
100 ml (3½ fl oz) light olive oil
2 spring onions, finely sliced or 2 tbsp snipped fresh chives
½ tsp caster sugar
salt and freshly ground black pepper, to season

* Cook the pasta according to the packet instructions, drain and set aside.
* Steam the carrot, broccoli, cauliflower and French beans for 2 minutes. Add the red pepper and courgette and continue to cook for a further 5 minutes. Add the sweetcorn for the last minute. Transfer the vegetables to a serving bowl and season with a little salt and pepper. Stir in the drained pasta and chicken, if using.
* To make the dressing, whisk the vinegar with the salt and pepper, then whisk in the oil a little at a time. Add the spring onions or chives and the sugar. Toss the pasta salad with the dressing.

☆ I make this salad using Animal Pasta, which is one of the organic pasta shapes in my Make Your Own range. Novelty pasta shapes tend to be popular with children. You can get them to name the animals as they eat them.

bacon and tomato spaghetti sauce

Fussy children often like bacon. Grilled smoked bacon gives this sauce a deliciously smoky flavour, but if you prefer you can use unsmoked. I prefer to use back bacon, but streaky bacon, which doesn't take as long to cook, would also work well. If your children like mushrooms then add 110 g (4 oz) halved button mushrooms and grill with the bacon.

8 rashers smoked bacon, rind removed, cut into 2.5-cm (1-in) pieces
2 × 400 g cans chopped tomatoes
½ tsp dried oregano
½ tsp sugar
a pinch of dried chilli flakes (optional)
300 g (10½ oz) spaghetti
freshly grated Parmesan, to serve

* Heat grill to high. Line a lipped baking sheet with foil. Grill the bacon for about 4 minutes then turn and grill for a further 4 minutes until cooked through and golden brown at the edges. Mix together the tomatoes, oregano, sugar and chilli flakes (if using) and pour over the bacon. Grill for a further 8–10 minutes, stirring 3–4 times, until the sauce has thickened slightly and is bubbling.
* Meanwhile, cook the spaghetti according to packet instructions and drain well. Season the sauce with pepper but go easy on the salt as bacon is usually quite salty. Serve the spaghetti with the sauce spooned over and sprinkled with grated Parmesan.

kiddie carbonara

A quick and easy way to make a tasty pasta sauce. Tailor-make it to your child's taste by adding different vegetables or even diced chicken or prawns instead of the ham.

170 g (6 oz) pasta (fusilli, bows or spaghetti)
55 g (2 oz) frozen peas
1 tbsp crème fraîche
2 tbsp fresh lemon juice
2 tbsp freshly grated Parmesan, plus a little to serve
2–4 slices ham, cut into strips

* Cook the pasta according to the packet instructions, adding the peas for the last 2 minutes of cooking time. Reserve a cupful of cooking water, then drain the pasta and return it to the pan.
* Stir the crème fraîche, lemon juice and Parmesan into the pasta. Add a splash of the cooking water if it becomes too dry. Stir in the ham. Season to taste and serve with extra Parmesan.

SUITABLE FOR FREEZING
PREPARATION TIME 15 MINUTES
COOKING TIME 1 HOUR
MAKES 6 PORTIONS

caroline's lasagne alfredo

Lasagne tends to be popular with children, so it's a good idea to combine the pasta itself with some other nutritious ingredients. This delicious lasagne is made with chicken and spinach. You can use fresh lasagne or the dried, no pre-cook variety – I prefer fresh.

250 g (9 oz) spinach, washed
9 sheets dried, no pre-cook lasagne
2 chicken breasts, about 110 g (4 oz) each, thinly sliced
FOR THE SAUCE
60 g (4 oz) butter
1 small onion, finely chopped
1 garlic clove, crushed
60 g (2 oz) plain flour
350 ml (12 fl oz) chicken stock
300 ml (10 fl oz) milk
110 g (4 oz) Cheddar, grated
50 g (2 oz) freshly grated Parmesan (reserve 4 tbsp for the topping)
salt, pepper and freshly grated nutmeg, to season

* Pre-heat the oven to 200°C/400°F/Gas 6. Melt the butter in a medium pan and sauté the onion for 5–6 minutes until softening and just starting to turn golden. Add the garlic and cook for 1 minute, then stir in the flour and cook for 1 minute. Remove from the heat and gradually stir in the stock and milk. Cook over a medium heat, stirring constantly until the sauce thickens and comes to a simmer. Remove from the heat, cool for a minute, then stir in the Cheddar and Parmesan and season well with salt, pepper and nutmeg.
* Cook the spinach in a large pan until wilted. Cool, then squeeze out as much liquid as possible and chop roughly.
* Put a thin layer of sauce in the bottom of a 24 cm × 15 cm (8 in × 5 in) ovenproof dish and add a layer of lasagne sheets. Scatter over half of the spinach and chicken, season with salt and pepper and spoon over one third of the sauce. Add a further layer of lasagne, and repeat layers of spinach, chicken, seasoning, sauce and lasagne. Top with the remaining sauce and sprinkle over the reserved Parmesan. Bake for 40–45 minutes until piping hot in the centre. Allow to stand for 15 minutes before serving.

i don't like...

anything green

Cheeky chicken

mini chicken patties

My Chicken and Apple Balls recipe in my first book, *Complete Baby and Toddler Meal Planner*, was created for my son Nicholas. He liked apples but wouldn't eat chicken, so I combined the two and made Chicken and Apple Ball finger food. It's good to find finger foods for children that are also nutritious and the apple combines with the chicken, giving it a lovely flavour and keeping it really moist.

½ red onion, finely chopped
½ medium carrot, coarsely grated
½ medium apple, peeled, cored and grated
3 tbsp sunflower or canola oil
½ tsp chopped fresh thyme
1 garlic clove, crushed
1 slice white bread, crusts removed
250 g (9 oz) minced chicken
½ crumbled chicken stock cube (for babies of 1 year and older)
salt and pepper, to taste

* In a large frying pan, sauté the onion, carrot and apple in 1 tablespoon of oil for 4 minutes. Stir in the thyme and garlic and cook for 1 minute. Remove from the heat and allow to cool slightly.
* Meanwhile, put the bread in a food processor and whiz into crumbs. Add the onion mixture, chicken and stock cube (if using) and combine for 1–2 minutes.
* Wipe out the frying pan with kitchen paper, then add the remaining 2 tablespoons of oil. Over a medium heat, drop dessertspoons of the chicken mixture into the pan, flattening the patties slightly with a spatula or the back of a fork until about ½ cm (¼ in) thick. Fry for around 1½ minutes each side in batches of 6 to 8 until golden brown and cooked through. These are good cooked on a griddle. Drain briefly on kitchen paper before serving.

☆ Suitable for freezing – put the patties on a baking sheet lined with cling film. Cover with more cling film and freeze until solid. When frozen, transfer to a freezer bag.

japanese-style chicken fillets

My kids like to eat this with edamame beans, which are being hailed as the new superfood and look like a cross between a broad bean and a pea. You can buy edamame beans frozen in packets. Lightly boil in salted water and squeeze the seeds into your mouth. I make a dip for the edamame that consists of 2 tablespoons of dark soy sauce mixed with half a tablespoon of mirin.

3 tbsp plain flour
2 eggs, lightly beaten
50 g (2 oz) fresh white breadcrumbs
450 g (1 lb) skinless chicken breasts
salt and freshly ground black pepper, to season

SAUCE
1 medium onion, peeled and thinly sliced
1 tbsp sunflower oil
4 spring onions, finely sliced
2 tbsp light soy sauce
100 ml (3½ fl oz) mirin
350 ml (12 fl oz) chicken stock

* Put the flour, beaten eggs and breadcrumbs into three shallow bowls. Cover the chicken breasts with cling film then pound with a mallet until about 1 cm (½ in) thick. Cut each one into 4 strips. Season with salt and freshly ground black pepper, then dip into the flour, then the egg and finally the breadcrumbs.
* To make the sauce, gently fry the onion in the sunflower oil, covered for about 5 minutes until very soft, then uncovered for 5 minutes more. Add the spring onions, soy sauce, mirin and stock. Simmer for 3 minutes.
* Fry the chicken strips in batches in a clean frying pan until golden and cooked through. Serve on a bed of rice with the sauce poured over.

☆ Ethnic-type recipes often work well with fussy children. I use mirin, a sweet Japanese cooking wine, quite a bit. It has a flavour that children like and is the key ingredient in Teriyaki sauce (see also Teriyaki Beef Skewers on page 142).

chinese chicken wraps

A tasty tortilla filling with an oriental flavour – I like the scrumptious mix of the mayonnaise and plum sauce and the crunch of the beansprouts. It might be fun to get your child involved in helping to assemble these. Even small children can help to mix up the filling.

2 tbsp mayonnaise
1 tbsp plum sauce
½ tsp dark soy sauce
½ tsp fresh lemon juice
a small handful of beansprouts
½ × 198 g tin sweetcorn
55 g (2 oz) cooked chicken
1 tortilla

* Mix together the mayonnaise, plum sauce, soy sauce and lemon juice. Stir in the beansprouts, sweetcorn and cooked chicken.
* Heat the tortilla for a few seconds in a microwave or a dry frying pan.
* Arrange the filling near one end of the tortilla then roll up. Cut the tortilla in half diagonally. You will need to wrap the end of each half in foil as the filling is quite wet and will otherwise slip out.

lara's chicken wraps

This is my daughter Lara's favourite recipe. Just like many children she gets fixated on one particular recipe and would like to eat it every day. She also enjoys assembling the wrap herself. I think that being involved in making their own food can encourage fussy eaters to try eating new things. You could also use strips of Maple-Glazed Griddled Chicken (page 120) inside these wraps.

2 skinned chicken breasts
1 tbsp sunflower oil
4 large flour tortillas
4 tbsp mayonnaise
a handful of shredded iceberg lettuce, shredded
4 tomatoes, seeded and cut into strips
salt and freshly ground black pepper, to season

MARINADE
1 tbsp olive oil
1 tbsp fresh lemon juice
1 garlic clove, lightly crushed
1 tbsp dark soy sauce
1 tbsp clear honey
½ tbsp brown sugar
2 tbsp sunflower oil

* Score the chicken with a sharp knife. Mix together all the ingredients for the marinade and marinate the chicken for about 30 minutes.
* Brush a griddle pan with oil. Remove the chicken from the marinade and, when the griddle is hot, griddle the chicken for approximately 4 minutes each side or until cooked through. Then cut into strips and set aside.

* Heat each tortilla for 10 seconds in a microwave or in a hot, dry, frying pan for 15 seconds, one at a time. Spread each one with 1 tablespoon of mayonnaise and arrange the chicken strips in a line down one side of the tortilla, about 4 cm (1½ in) from the edge the tortilla, with parallel lines of shredded lettuce down one side and tomato strips down the other. Roll up and cut each tortilla in half and wrap in foil to serve.

☆ You can marinate and cook the chicken in advance if you like. If you don't have time to cook the chicken, you can buy some marinated cooked chicken and use that instead.

PREPARATION TIME 5 MINUTES
COKING TIME 10 MINUTES
MAKES 4 PORTIONS

ten-minute chicken noodle soup

Children tend to like chicken noodle soup, so here's a quick and easy version for you to make at home.

1 medium carrot, diced
1 litre (1¾ pints) good-quality chicken stock
½ tsp fresh thyme leaves
50 g (2 oz) fine noodles (such as vermicelli), broken into pieces
60 g (2¼ oz) cooked chicken, shredded
4 tbsp frozen peas
salt and freshly ground pepper, to season

* Put the carrot, stock and thyme in a medium-sized pan. Bring to the boil and add the noodles. Simmer for 5 minutes or until the noodles are just cooked.
* Add the chicken and frozen peas. Bring back to the simmer and cook for a further minute. Season to taste.

i don't like...

naked chicken

without breadcrumbs

japanese chicken salad

A delicious chicken salad made with Thai Jasmine rice. You can buy this in most supermarkets – it's quite similar to sushi rice. The crunchy texture of the cucumber and red pepper contrasts well with the rice and the dressing gives the salad a delicious flavour that is not too strong, so should attract fussy eaters. This would make a good addition to your child's lunchbox.

110 g (4 oz) Thai Jasmine rice
⅓ cucumber
3 spring onions, sliced
½ red pepper, diced
85 g (3 oz) cooked chicken, diced
¼ avocado, diced (optional)
salt and pepper, to taste

DRESSING
2 tbsp rice wine vinegar
1 tbsp caster sugar
½ tbsp sunflower oil

* Put the rice in a large pan with plenty of cold water and a pinch of salt. Bring to the boil and simmer for 12–15 minutes until the rice is just tender. Drain and leave to stand in a sieve for 15 minutes, stirring halfway through, then transfer to a bowl.
* To make the dressing, gently warm the rice wine vinegar and sugar until the sugar has dissolved. Add the sunflower oil and stir into the rice. Leave until cold and refrigerate (if using for a lunchbox).
* Cut the cucumber in half lengthways and scoop out the seeds with a teaspoon. Dice the flesh. Stir into the dressed rice with the spring onions, pepper, chicken and avocado (if using) and season to taste.

nasi goreng: indonesian fried rice

Indonesians use Kecap Manis, a sweetened soy sauce. If you have this, then use 3 tablespoons rather than the soy sauce and brown sugar. You can add extra vegetables with the pepper, such as broccoli florets, sliced baby sweetcorn or mangetout.

2 eggs
1 tbsp sunflower oil
1 medium onion, thinly sliced
¼ red pepper, diced
1 garlic clove, crushed
½ tsp grated fresh ginger
450 g (1 lb) cold cooked rice (200 g/7 oz uncooked weight)
50 g (2 oz) frozen peas
170 g (6 oz) cooked chicken, shredded
75 g (2½ oz) cooked prawns
2 tbsp dark soy sauce
1 tbsp soft brown sugar
4 small or 2 large spring onions, thinly sliced
salt and freshly ground black pepper, to taste
a handful of fresh coriander leaves, to serve (optional)
1 lime, quartered, to serve (optional)

* Beat the eggs with a pinch of salt and a few grindings of black pepper. Heat 1 teaspoon of the oil in a wok and when sizzling add the eggs. Cook for 1–2 minutes (the eggs may puff a bit), until golden on the underside, then flip the omelette over and cook for another minute until set. Transfer to a plate and cut into small pieces.
* Heat the remaining oil in the wok and stir fry the onion for 4 minutes, add the pepper, garlic and ginger, and cook for a further 2–3 minutes until the onion is golden. Add the cooked rice, peas, chicken and prawns and stir fry for a further 5 minutes, until everything is hot.
* Mix the soy sauce and brown sugar together and stir through the rice, along with the pieces of omelette. Remove from the heat and stir in the spring onions. Serve with coriander leaves scattered on top and lime wedges to squeeze over.

monday-night risotto

In my house this is often known as Monday Night Risotto, as it is a good way to use up leftover roast chicken. This method gives a deliciously creamy risotto.

50 g (2 oz) butter
2 large shallots or 2 small onions, finely chopped
1 garlic clove, crushed
200 g (7 oz) risotto rice (e.g. arborio)
1.25 litres (2 pints) hot chicken stock, plus more as necessary
100 g (4 oz) cooked chicken
75 g (3 oz) frozen peas
25 g (1 oz) grated Parmesan, plus extra to serve
2 tbsp lemon juice
½ tbsp chopped flatleaf parsley (optional)
salt and freshly ground black pepper, to season

* Melt the butter and gently cook the shallots or onions for 5 minutes, until soft but not coloured. Add the garlic and rice and cook for 2 minutes, until the rice starts to turn translucent.
* Put the stock in a large saucepan and bring to the boil. Keep on a very low heat while you are making the risotto. Add the hot stock to the rice a ladleful at a time, allowing the rice to absorb all the stock before adding any more. Continue to add the stock gradually, stirring often for about 20 minutes (it might take a little longer) until the rice is tender and creamy but the grains are still firm in the centre. Make sure you have some stock left in the pan (about 100 ml/3 fl oz).
* Add the chicken, peas and Parmesan and cook, stirring, for 2 minutes. Mix in the lemon zest and juice plus enough of the remaining stock to give a loose but not sloppy consistency. Add extra stock if necessary, as the absorption will differ according to the type of rice.
* Remove from the heat and stir in the parsley, then season to taste with salt and pepper. Serve with extra grated Parmesan.

maple-glazed griddled chicken

This slightly sweet combination of ketchup, maple syrup and smoked paprika should tempt fussy eaters. The paprika gives the chicken a rich flavour and orange hue. Sweet smoked paprika is available in some supermarkets, Spanish delicatessens and also online from delicioso.co.uk. Be careful not to use hot paprika by mistake!

4 skinned chicken breasts
light olive oil, for griddling

MARINADE
5 tbsp vegetable oil
5 tbsp tomato ketchup
3 tbsp maple syrup
3 tsp sweet smoked paprika

* First, flatten the chicken. One good way to do so is to slit one side of a plastic freezer bag so that you can position the meat inside then cover with the plastic. Use a heavy smooth-sided mallet to pound the chicken, working from the middle outwards to a uniform thickness. Or cover with cling film and bash a few times with a mallet.
* Whisk together the vegetable oil, ketchup, maple syrup and paprika, pour over the chicken and leave to marinate for a couple of hours.
* Heat the griddle, brush with a little olive oil and griddle the chicken for about 4 minutes on each side or until cooked through, basting occasionally. Pour over any extra juices to serve.

☆ I like to cook marinated chicken on the griddle. A griddle is a healthy way of cooking as it uses little fat and keeps the chicken tender and moist. You can also griddle vegetables, such as sliced courgettes, mangetout and sweet peppers. You could use an ordinary griddle, but one of the best pieces of kitchen equipment that I have is a contact griddle and grill. I use it all the time – it functions as an open griddle, open indoor grill, contact grill and panini press and it works for everything from chicken and hamburgers to fish and vegetables. It griddles both sides of the chicken at once, cutting the cooking time in half.

sticky chicken

Mrs Ball started making chutney to her mother's secret recipe when she moved to Johannesburg with her seven children. Her friends and family loved it so much that her chutney business went from selling about 24 bottles a day in 1918, to over 8000 bottles a day within only a few years. In the early 1970s, Brooke Bond Oxo took over the business, and Mrs Ball's chutney is now exported to Britain. Sadly, Mrs Ball died in 1962 at the age of 92, when three youths assaulted her for a small purse of money as she sat on the front deck of her house in Fish Hoek, near Cape Town.

8 chicken thighs, totalling about 1 kg (2 lb 4 oz), on the bone, skin on,
or 4 chicken breasts, on the bone
salt and freshly ground black pepper, to season
MARINADE
8 tbsp Mrs Ball's Original Recipe Chutney (available in good supermarkets and delis)
2 tbsp fresh lemon juice
2 tbsp Worcestershire sauce
2 tbsp dark soy sauce
4 tbsp tomato ketchup
1 tbsp clear honey
2 tbsp olive oil

* Mix the marinade ingredients together in a bowl. Score each chicken thigh two or three times and place in an ovenproof dish. Pour over the marinade and season. Alternatively marinate in a large freezer bag. Leave to marinate for at least 30 minutes.
* Pre-heat a grill to high. Transfer the chicken to a grill rack and cook for 30 minutes, turning every 5 minutes.
* If you use 4 chicken breasts (on the bone, skin on) instead, marinate in the usual way, then cover in foil and roast at 200°C/400°F/Gas 6 for 20 minutes. Uncover and cook for a further 20 minutes. For an extra-crispy skin, pop under the grill for a final couple of minutes before serving.

chicken satay skewers

This is a good recipe if you have a fussy eater who likes peanut butter – they will appreciate the flavour, and it's fun eating chicken off a skewer. It is also good made with chicken thigh meat, as it's moist and tender, so you could substitute two large chicken thighs for the chicken breast.

1 large skinned chicken breast, cut into 1-cm (½-in) cubes
MARINADE
1 tbsp peanut butter
1 tbsp coconut cream
½ tsp medium curry paste (Patak's Balti is worth trying)
1 tsp fresh lime juice
a large pinch of salt or ¼ tsp fish sauce
¼ tsp sugar
1 tbsp water

* You will need 6 bamboo skewers.
* Put the marinade ingredients in a bowl and mix to combine. Add the chicken and toss to coat. Marinate for at least 1 hour and preferably overnight.
* Soak the 6 bamboo skewers in water. Pre-heat the grill to high. Thread 4–5 pieces of chicken on to each skewer. Grill for 3–4 minutes on each side or until cooked through. Alternatively, cook on a griddle.

chicken nuggets with dipping sauces

Japanese honey panko breadcrumbs are particularly good for this. You can buy these in Japanese food shops or some large supermarkets. Otherwise use plain, dried breadcrumbs. Marinating chicken in buttermilk gives it a delicious flavour and keeps it nice and tender. Get the kids to help whip up the fillings.

350 g (12 oz) skinless and boneless chicken breasts (approx. 3 chicken breasts), cut into 2.5-cm (1-in) pieces
4 tbsp sunflower oil, for frying

MARINADE
200 ml (7 fl oz) buttermilk
1 tbsp fresh lemon juice
1 tsp Worcestershire Sauce
1 tsp soy sauce
¼ tsp paprika

COATING
100 g (3½ oz) plain flour
1 egg, beaten with 1 tbsp water
75 g (2½ oz) dry breadcrumbs or honey panko breadcrumbs
45 g (1½ oz) freshly grated Parmesan
salt and pepper, to season

* Combine the marinade ingredients and soak the chicken pieces for 2 hours.
* Put the flour on a large plate. Beat the egg with the water and season with salt and pepper. Mix the breadcrumbs and Parmesan on a large plate. Remove chicken cubes from the marinade, shaking off any excess, and toss them in the flour. Then dip the cubes in the egg mixture and roll in the breadcrumbs

* Heat the oil in a large frying pan and sauté the chicken nuggets for 2–3 minutes on each side until golden and cooked through, turning occasionally. Alternatively, pre-heat oven to 200°C/400°F/Gas 6. Put the chicken nuggets on a generously oiled large baking sheet and bake for 18–20 minutes until the coating is crisp and the chicken cooked.
* While the nuggets are baking you can whip up these easy dips, by simply mixing the ingredients in a bowl:

BBQ DIP
6 tbsp tomato ketchup
2 tbsp maple syrup
½ tsp Worcestershire sauce
½ tsp soy sauce
2–3 drops Tabasco sauce (optional)

HONEY-MUSTARD DIP
4 tbsp mayonnaise
1 tsp wholegrain Dijon mustard
1½ tsp clear honey
1 tsp cold water

chicken paillard with rocket & cherry tomatoes

I do quite a lot of work with restaurants, trying to introduce healthier meals to children. This is one of the dishes available at London's Villandry, a foodstore with restaurants, where I have helped design the children's menu. It's very popular, which just goes to show that chicken doesn't always have to be covered in breadcrumbs.

2 skinned chicken breasts, batted out to 5 mm (¼ in) thickness
a little olive oil, for griddling

MARINADE
1 garlic clove, finely chopped
1 tsp finely chopped fresh thyme
2 tbsp olive oil
salt and freshly ground black pepper

DRESSING
1 tbsp light olive oil
1 tsp balsamic vinegar
a pinch of sugar
a small bunch of rocket
8 cherry tomatoes salt and freshly ground black pepper, to season

* Cover the chicken breasts with cling film or greaseproof paper and flatten with a mallet. Whisk together the chopped garlic, thyme, olive oil and seasoning, and marinade the chicken for at least 20 minutes.
* Heat a griddle and brush with a little oil. Remove the chicken from the marinade and griddle for about 4 minutes on each side or until cooked through. If you have a contact griddle, you can close the lid and cook the chicken on both sides at the same time, cutting the cooking time in half.
* To make the dressing, mix the olive oil and balsamic vinegar and season with a little sugar, salt and pepper. Toss with the rocket and cherry tomatoes and serve as a side dish to the chicken.

yummy chicken quesadillas

A quesadilla is what you get when you cook ingredients inside a tortilla. The filling can be wrapped inside the tortilla by folding it over, or it can be sandwiched between two tortillas, as in the Vegetable Quesadillas on page 50. I find that children tend to eat food that they would never otherwise eat if it's inside tortillas.

½ tbsp sunflower oil
1 skinless chicken breast, sliced into small strips
½ onion, sliced
¼ red pepper, cut into thin slices
1 tbsp balsamic vinegar
½ tsp brown sugar
2 tbsp salsa
2 large tortillas
55 g (2 oz) Cheddar, grated

* Pre-heat a grill to high. Heat the oil in a wok or large frying pan and stir fry the chicken for 2 minutes. Add the onion and cook for 2 minutes. Add the pepper and cook for 2–3 minutes. Add the balsamic vinegar and sugar and cook for 1 minute.
* Spread 1 tablespoon of salsa over half of each tortilla and sprinkle over half the Cheddar. Divide the chicken mixture between the two tortillas and sprinkle with the rest of the cheese. Roll up and secure with a cocktail stick.
* Grill for 1½–2 minutes on each side to warm the tortilla and melt the cheese.

TIP:
A hungry child is a less fussy child so time snacks so that they are not too close to mealtimes. When they come home from school is a time when your child is usually starving so have some good food prepared like these quesadillas instead of giving them crisps or chocolate biscuits.

chicken in tomato and sweet pepper sauce

This is a delicious sauce that goes really well with chicken. The red onions and roasted red peppers add a sweetness that children like to the tomato sauce. Serve with fluffy white rice.

4 chicken breasts, about 110 g (4 oz) each
1½ tsp olive oil
SWEET PEPPER SAUCE
2 large red peppers, seeded and cored
2 medium red onions, chopped
1 garlic clove, crushed
1 tbsp olive oil
1 × 400 g can tomatoes
150 ml (5 fl oz) vegetable stock
1 tbsp butter
salt and pepper, to season

* Pre-heat the grill to high. Put the peppers cut-side down on a grill tray, lined with foil if you like. Grill for 15–20 minutes until the skin is black and blistered. Meanwhile, cook the onions and garlic gently in olive oil in a casserole dish until soft but not coloured.
* Cover the chicken breasts with cling film and bash with a mallet to flatten. Heat the griddle, brush with a little olive oil and griddle the chicken for about 4 minutes on each side or until cooked through.
* Remove the peppers from the grill and cool for 5 minutes. When cool enough to handle, remove the skins and chop roughly. Add to the onions with the tomatoes and vegetable stock. Bring to a simmer, breaking up the tomatoes with a spoon. Add the chicken. Cook for 20–25 minutes, turning the chicken halfway through.
* Blend the sauce until smooth. Stir in the butter and season. Remove the chicken from the casserole and cut into slices, spoon over the sauce and serve with fluffy white rice.

chicken balls in tomato sauce

Meatballs and chicken balls tend to be popular and this recipe is good made with minced beef, chicken or turkey. It also freezes well, so it's good to keep a stock of this for times when the pantry is bare.

1 tbsp flour, to dust hands
3 tbsp sunflower oil, for frying

CHICKEN BALLS
2 tbsp olive oil
1 medium onion, finely chopped
40 g (1½ oz) white breadcrumbs
(approx. 2 slices)
55 ml (2 fl oz) milk
250 g (9 oz) chicken or turkey mince
1 small apple, peeled and grated
1 tsp fresh thyme leaves
½ tsp salt and freshly ground
black pepper

TOMATO SAUCE
1 tbsp olive oil
1 small red onion, finely chopped
1 garlic clove, crushed
1 × 400 g (14 oz) can chopped
   tomatoes
1 tbsp tomato ketchup
1 tsp brown sugar
4 tbsp water
salt and freshly ground black
   pepper, to season

* To make the chicken balls, heat the oil in a pan and fry the onion gently for about 10 minutes until softened. Meanwhile soak the breadcrumbs in milk for 10 minutes in a large bowl.
* Add the chicken or turkey mince, grated apple, thyme, sautéed onion, salt and black pepper to the soaked breadcrumbs and mix together. Using floured hands, form teaspoonfuls of the mixture into small balls. Heat the sunflower oil in a frying pan and brown the meatballs. They will be cooked again in the sauce, so cook for only about 5 minutes.
* To make the tomato sauce, heat the olive oil and sauté the red onion for 5 minutes. Add the garlic and cook for 1 minute. Add the remaining ingredients and season with salt and pepper. Bring to a simmer and cook for 10 minutes. Add 2 tablespoons of extra water if the sauce thickens too much.
* Add the browned chicken balls to the sauce and cook for about 10 minutes. Serve with rice.

chicken drumsticks with barbecue sauce

Chicken drumsticks with a tasty barbecue sauce are popular with my three children. They can eat two each, but it really depends how large the drumsticks are. I score the drumsticks a few times to make sure that the meat is cooked all the way through.

6 chicken drumsticks

MARINADE
3 tbsp tomato ketchup
1 tbsp sunflower oil
1 tbsp rice wine vinegar
1 tbsp dark soy sauce
2 tbsp honey
1 tsp paprika
1 garlic clove, crushed

* Wash the chicken drumsticks and pat dry with kitchen paper. Score each one three times using a sharp knife.
* Thoroughly mix together all the ingredients for the marinade. Coat the drumsticks in the marinade and leave to marinate for at least 30 minutes or overnight.
* Pre-heat the oven to 200°C/400°F/Gas 6. Line a baking sheet or roasting tin with foil. Place the drumsticks on the sheet/tin together with the marinade. Roast for 35–40 minutes or until the chicken is thoroughly cooked.

the one-bowl meal

This is a really yummy chicken soup and perfect for when you have leftover roast chicken. With the chicken, rice and vegetables it makes a meal in itself and some fussy eaters are much happier eating soup.

½ medium onion, chopped
1 tbsp olive oil
1 medium carrot, diced
650 ml (20 fl oz) good chicken stock
½ tsp fresh thyme leaves
50 g (2 oz) frozen peas
85 g (3 oz) drained canned sweetcorn
110 g (4 oz) cooked chicken
170 g (6 oz) cooked rice (55 g/2 oz uncooked)
salt and pepper, to season

* Sauté the onion in the oil gently for about 5 minutes. Add the carrot, stock and thyme and simmer for 4–5 minutes or until the carrot softens. Add the peas and sweetcorn and simmer for 3 minutes.
* Shred the chicken into pieces and add to the soup together with the cooked rice and simmer for 2 minutes to reheat. Season with a little salt and pepper.

MMM...eat

meatballs with tomato sauce

These mini meatballs are delicious served on a bed of rice. They are simple to prepare and make a wonderful family meal. They also work well as finger food, served on their own without the sauce.

MEATBALLS

3 tbsp vegetable oil
1 onion, finely chopped
50 g (2 oz) red pepper, diced
450 g (1 lb) lean minced beef
1 apple, peeled and grated
50 g (2 oz) fresh white breadcrumbs
1 tbsp chopped fresh parsley
1 chicken stock cube, finely crumbled
2 tbsp cold water
salt and freshly ground black pepper
plain flour, for dusting

TOMATO SAUCE

1 tbsp olive oil
1 medium red onion, finely chopped
1 garlic clove, crushed
600 g (1 lb 5 oz) chopped tomatoes (1 × 400 g + 1 × 200 g can)
1½ tbsp tomato ketchup
6 tbsp water
salt and freshly ground black pepper, to season

* To make the meatballs, heat 1 tablespoon of vegetable oil in a pan and sauté the onion and red pepper for about 5 minutes or until softened. Mix together with all the other ingredients for the meatballs and chop for a few seconds in a food processor. Using floured hands, form the mixture into about 20 meatballs. Heat the rest of the vegetable oil in a frying pan and sauté the meatballs, turning occasionally, for about 5 minutes, until browned and sealed.
* Meanwhile, to make the sauce, heat the olive oil and sauté the red onion for 5 minutes. Add the garlic and cook for 1 minute. Add the remaining ingredients and season with salt and pepper. Bring to a simmer and cook for 5 minutes. Add a little more water if the sauce thickens too much. Add the meatballs, half cover with a lid and simmer, stirring occasionally, for about 10 minutes or until cooked through. You need to be careful when stirring the meatballs into the sauce as if you are too vigorous they may break up. Serve with rice.

annabel's yummy burgers

Making your own healthy junk food is one way to encourage fussy eaters to eat better-quality food. Adding tomato chutney to burgers gives them a delicious flavour. My children love these. Serve them on their own or in a bun with some salad.

1 medium red onion, chopped
3 tbsp sunflower oil
1 garlic clove, crushed
½ tsp thyme leaves
2 slices white bread, crusts removed
250 g (9 oz) minced beef
3 tbsp tomato chutney (or you could use tomato relish)
salt and freshly ground black pepper
1–2 tbsp flour, for dusting

✳ Sauté the onion in 1 tablespoon of sunflower oil for 5–6 minutes until soft. Add the garlic and thyme and cook for 1 minute. Tear the bread into pieces and put in a food processor with the onion mixture and blitz.
✳ If you want a really smooth texture, pulse all the ingredients together in the food processor for a few seconds. If not, combine all the ingredients in a bowl and season to taste. Form the mixture into 4 burgers using flour-dusted hands.
✳ For the best flavour, I like to cook these on a contact griddle that does both sides at once – this method of cooking also halves the cooking time. Alternatively, fry the burgers in the remaining oil for 4–5 minutes on each side over a medium-to-low heat. If you fry over a high heat, because of the sugar in the tomato chutney the burgers have a tendency to burn.

☆ If you want to freeze burgers, it's best to do so uncooked on a tray lined with cling film. When they are frozen, wrap them individually in cling film. You can then remove them and use as many as you like.

alison's favourite shepherd's pie

Dr Alison French is a specialist registrar in Paediatrics and Child Health. She helps me answer all the e-mails I receive every day via my website. Alison's children, Amelie and Ben, love this recipe.

700 g (1 lb 9 oz) Maris Piper potatoes, peeled
40 g (1 ½ oz) unsalted butter
6 tbsp milk
1 large or 2 small onions
2 medium carrots
1 large or 2 small courgettes
½ red pepper
1 tbsp olive oil
1 garlic clove, crushed
500 g (1 lb 2 oz) lamb mince (I use organic as it tastes much nicer)
1 tsp cinnamon
1 tsp dried mixed herbs
1 tsp caster sugar
freshly ground black pepper
1 tbsp plain flour
300 ml (10 fl oz) hot beef stock
1 tbsp double tomato purée
50 g (2 oz) mild Cheddar, grated

* Boil the potatoes until soft and floury (about 15 minutes) and then drain. Mash with the butter and milk and set aside
* Heat the olive oil in a large pan. Finely chop the onion, carrot, courgette and red pepper in a food processor and sauté in the oil for 4 minutes until soft but not browned. Add the garlic and cook for 1 minute. Stir in the lamb mince and turn up the heat. When the meat is browned, add the cinnamon, herbs, sugar, a little freshly ground black pepper and flour and stir well. Add the tomato purée to the hot stock and add to the pan. Stir well, and simmer for about 10 minutes.
* Pre-heat the oven to 180°C/350°F/Gas 4. Spoon the meat into a large, clear casserole or deep pie dish. Top the meat mixture with the mashed potatoes and fork over until it is smooth. Sprinkle over the cheese and bake for about 30 minutes in centre of the oven until the top is brown, and the meat is bubbling.

luscious lamb koftas

If your child just won't sit still long enough to eat anything, it might be a good idea to try finger food. Iron is the most common nutritional deficiency in young children, so it's good to make finger foods such as these koftas as meat provides the best source of iron, which is important for growth and development and crucial in the production of healthy red blood cells, which carry oxygen around the body including to the brain. A deficiency of iron often leads to lack of concentration and tiredness and ensuring that your child gets enough iron can markedly improve academic performance.

2 onions, chopped
1 tbsp olive oil
500 g (1 lb 2 oz) minced lamb
80 g (3 oz) fresh breadcrumbs
2 tbsp chopped coriander
2 tbsp chopped fresh parsley
1 tbsp mild curry powder
2 tsp ground cumin
1 lightly beaten egg
1 beef stock cube, crumbled
1 tsp sugar
salt and pepper, to season
plain flour, for rolling
vegetable oil, for frying

TO SERVE
7 standard-size pitta breads
Greek yoghurt
14 slices tomato
14 slices cucumber

* Sauté one of the onions in the oil until softened. Then mix together the sautéed onion, raw onion, minced lamb and all the remaining kofta ingredients (except the flour and vegetable oil). Transfer to a food processor and chop for few seconds. Form the mixture into 14 koftas (short, fat sausage shapes), roll in flour and sauté until golden and cooked through.
* Cut the pitta pockets in half. Spoon a little yoghurt into each pocket and stuff each one with a lamb kofta, a slice of cucumber and a slice of tomato. If you prefer, serve without pitta pockets and maybe some couscous or rice (as well as the yoghurt and salad).

teriyaki beef skewers

The beauty of this is that it is so quick and easy to prepare, and the teriyaki marinade may tempt children who aren't keen on red meat. When grating ginger, grate with the grain – you will see what I mean if you try to do it the other way. Mirin is the key ingredient used to make teriyaki sauce. It is a sweet Japanese rice wine used for cooking. You can buy it in some supermarkets and also Asian food stores.

sirloin steak, about 200 g (7 oz), fat removed and cut into 1-cm (½-in) cubes
(or use fillet steak – tail fillet is less expensive)
TERIYAKI SAUCE
1 tbsp dark soy sauce
1 tbsp clear honey
1 tsp mirin
¼ tsp grated fresh ginger
1 tsp sesame oil
1 tsp sunflower oil

* You will need 4 bamboo skewers.
* To make the Teriyaki sauce, put the soy sauce, honey and mirin in a medium-size pan. Bring to the boil and cook for 30 seconds (or for 1 minute in a small pan). Allow to cool, then stir in the ginger and oils. Toss the cubed beef in a bowl with the marinade (it is quite sticky) and marinate for 1 hour or overnight. Meanwhile, soak four bamboo skewers in water.
* Pre-heat the grill to high. Remove the meat from the marinade and thread on to the skewers. Place the skewered meat on a baking sheet lined with foil. Baste with some of the marinade left in the bowl and grill for 2 minutes. Turn, baste with the marinade and grill again for 2 minutes. Baste once more with the marinade and juices collecting in the foil and grill a minute longer. Allow to cool slightly before serving. Alternatively, you could cook these on a griddle.

☆ To make another good teriyaki marinade, put 1 tbsp soy sauce, 2 tbsp sake, 2 tbsp mirin and 1 tbsp caster sugar in a small pan, and stir until the sugar has dissolved.

i don't like...

meat that's
not a burger
☹

-takes all Day
to chew

mini meatloaves

Mini portions are always more attractive to children, so try making mini meatloaves in a muffin pan. In fact you can also make tiny bite-sized meatloaves in mini muffin trays.

½ onion finely chopped
½ tbsp olive oil, plus extra for greasing
½ tsp chopped fresh thyme
2 slices white bread, crusts removed
250 g (9 oz) minced lean beef
3 tbsp tomato ketchup
1 tsp Worcestershire sauce
4 tbsp milk
½ tsp salt
black pepper, to taste
1 quantity Annabel's Secret Tomato Sauce (page 45) or your favourite tomato sauce

* Pre-heat the oven to 200°C/400°F/Gas 6. Sauté the onion in the olive oil for 5 minutes, then stir in the thyme. Remove from the heat and leave to cool slightly. Meanwhile, put the bread in the bowl of a food processor and whiz into crumbs. Add all the remaining ingredients including the sautéed onion (and black pepper to taste, but not the Tomato Sauce) and whiz for 1–2 minutes until combined.
* Lightly grease 2 mini-muffin pans or 1 ordinary muffin pan. For finger-size mini meatloaves put 1 tablespoonful in each cup of a mini-muffin pan. For the larger meatloaves put 2 tablespoonfuls in each cup of a muffin tray.
* Bake for 15 minutes for the mini muffins and 20 minutes for the ordinary muffin size. Remove from the tins with a spatula and serve with the Annabel's Secret Tomato Sauce (page 45).

☆ Freezing instructions are the same as for the Mini Chicken Patties (page 110). Defrost overnight in the fridge or for 1–2 hours at room temperature. You can reheat in the microwave or oven.

PREPARATION TIME 20 MINUTES
COOKING TIME 25 MINUTES
MAKES 5 PORTIONS
SUITABLE FOR FREEZING

swedish meatballs

50 g (2 oz) white bread (approx. 2 slices), crusts removed
4 tbsp milk
150 g (5¼ oz) onion, finely chopped
2 tbsp sunflower oil
110 g (4 oz) beef mince
110 g (4 oz) pork mince
¼ tsp grated nutmeg
1 egg yolk
a little salt and freshly ground black pepper, to season
1 tbsp plain flour, for dusting
SAUCE
20 g (¾ oz) butter
20 g (¾ oz) plain flour
300 ml (10 fl oz) good-quality beef stock
100 ml (3 fl oz) double cream
salt and freshly ground black pepper, to season

* Pre-heat oven to 200°C/400°F/Gas 6. Tear the bread into 1-cm (½-in) pieces and put in a bowl with the milk. Leave to soak for 10 minutes.
* Put the onion in a large pan with 1 tablespoon of the oil and sauté for 5–6 minutes over a medium heat, until the onion is translucent. Transfer roughly two thirds of the onion to a large bowl and add the milky bread, mince, nutmeg and egg yolk. Season well with the salt and pepper then mix until thoroughly combined (for a smoother texture, mix everything in a food processor).
* Put the remaining tablespoon of oil on a large baking sheet. Take heaped teaspoons of the meatball mixture and roll into about 25 balls using the palms of your hands – dust your hands with the flour to prevent the meatballs from sticking. Put the meatballs on the oiled baking sheet and bake for 20 minutes, turning halfway through.
* Meanwhile, make the sauce. Add the butter to the onion left in the saucepan. Melt over a low heat and stir in the flour. Cook gently for 2 minutes then remove from the heat and stir in the beef stock a little at a time until you have a smooth sauce. Stir in the cream. Return the pan to a medium heat and cook, stirring, for 7–8 minutes until the sauce has come up to boiling point and thickened slightly. Season to taste with salt and black pepper. Add the meatballs before serving.

sticky bbq ribs

These ribs make delicious finger food, and the added attraction is the sticky mess you get into chewing on them, so have the wet wipes handy.

1.25 kg (2 lb 12 oz) spare ribs
salt and freshly ground black pepper, to season

BBQ SAUCE

1 small red onion, chopped
1 tbsp olive oil
1 garlic clove, crushed
150 ml (5 fl oz) tomato ketchup
100 ml (3½ fl oz) fresh orange juice
4 tbsp clear honey
1 tbsp dark soy sauce
2 tsp Worcestershire sauce

* Pre-heat the oven to 170°C/325°F/Gas 3. In a frying pan, sauté the onion in the oil for 5 minutes until soft. Add the garlic and cook for 1 minute, then add the remaining sauce ingredients, bring up to a simmer and cook for 1 minute. Allow to cool slightly, then whiz together in a blender.
* Put the ribs in a large roasting tin (line with foil for easier clean-up) and season with salt and pepper. Pour over the sauce and toss the ribs to coat. Cover with foil and cook for 30 minutes. Increase the oven temperature to 200°C/400°F/Gas 6, uncover the ribs and cook for a further 30 minutes, turning over halfway. Transfer to a plate and allow to cool slightly before serving.
* Alternatively you can grill or BBQ the ribs – season and cook with a medium-hot grill or coals for 10 minutes on each side. Brush the ribs with some of the sauce then turn and grill or BBQ for 5 minutes. Repeat 3–4 times until the ribs are cooked through, with a sticky coating.

☆ You can pop some medium-sized baking potatoes into the oven at the same time as the ribs for a perfect accompaniment.

pork medallions with caramelized apples

If your children eat chicken then they should be tempted by pork, the other 'white meat'. The sweet caramelized apples will also whet tricky appetites and are a slightly more sophisticated version of apple sauce. You could use 4 medium-sized boneless pork loin chops (cook for 6–7 minutes each side) instead of fillet if you prefer.

450 g (1 lb) pork tenderloin fillet, trimmed
1 tbsp olive oil
2 tbsp cider vinegar
100 ml (3½ fl oz) vegetable or chicken stock
2 tbsp double cream
salt and pepper, to season
CARAMELIZED APPLES
15 g (½ oz) butter
1 large eating apple (e.g. Fuji), peeled, cored and cut into 12 wedges
1 tbsp granulated sugar
1 tbsp water

* To make the medallions, cut the fillet into 8 pieces and lay cut-side down between two pieces of cling film. Tap the pork with a rolling pin into medallions around 1.5 cm (½ in) thick.
* Heat the oil in a large frying pan. Season the pork medallions with salt and pepper and fry over a medium–high heat for around 3 minutes on each side, until just cooked through (be careful not to overcook or they will become dry). Transfer to a dish. Add the cider vinegar to the frying pan and boil for 1 minute, until almost evaporated. Add the stock and boil for 2–3 minutes, until reduced by half. Stir in the cream, pour the sauce over the pork medallions and keep warm in a low oven.
* Wipe out the frying pan with kitchen paper and add the butter. Heat until foaming then add the apple and cook over a medium–high heat for around 2 minutes on each side, until starting to turn golden brown. Sprinkle over the sugar and water and cook, stirring, for a further minute or two, until the apples are coated in a thin caramel. Serve with the pork.

lamb lollipops

Lamb cutlets make great finger food,
as they come with their own little 'sticks'.
If the glaze becomes too thick when cool,
warm it gently again before brushing on
the lamb.

1 tbsp redcurrant jelly
1 tsp fresh orange juice
a small pinch of ground cinnamon
(optional)
6 French-trimmed lamb cutlets
salt and pepper, to season

* Pre-heat the grill to high. Put the
redcurrant jelly, orange juice and cinnamon
in a small pan and heat until the jelly has
melted. Bring to the boil and cook for
around 15 seconds, then set aside to cool
and thicken slightly.
* Season the lamb with salt and pepper
and grill for 3–4 minutes on each side. Cool
slightly, then brush with the redcurrant
glaze before serving.

sloppy joe

Sloppy Joe is a hot sandwich, popular in
the US, composed of minced beef seasoned
with tomato sauce and served on a bun.
The term 'sloppy' comes from the fact that
eating it can be a little messy with the meat
sauce spilling out if you are not careful. You
could also mix this tasty sauce with rice.

1 tbsp sunflower oil
½ onion, chopped
1 small carrot, diced
½ stick celery, diced
⅛ red pepper, diced
300 g (10½ oz) minced beef or turkey
1 × 400 g can chopped tomatoes
100 ml (3½ fl oz) chicken stock
2 tsp red wine vinegar
2 tsp Worcestershire sauce
1 tsp brown sugar
1 tbsp tomato ketchup
a few drops of Tabasco sauce
salt and pepper, to season

* Heat the oil in a large frying pan and
sauté the vegetables for 5–6 minutes. Add
the minced beef or turkey and cook for 3–4
minutes until slightly browned. Add all the
other ingredients and simmer for 10
minutes. If dry, add an extra 50 ml (2 fl oz)
chicken stock. Season with salt and pepper.
Serve on a toasted hamburger bun.

gluten free
and georgeous

gluten

As food intolerances become more common, I find that many people are looking for recipes that avoid wheat or are suitable for coeliacs. It can be a challenge to cook for children who have to avoid wheat or gluten, as they shouldn't feel as if they are missing out on family meals or treats, and it's even more of a struggle if your child is a fussy eater. For this chapter I have created a collection of recipes that can be enjoyed by the whole family.

While you can buy a good variety of gluten-free foods, many contain additives and preservatives, and more often than not they just don't taste very good. The Coeliac Society will provide you with an up-to-date list of gluten-free foods.

Coeliac disease used to be considered rare, but now the frequency can be as high as 1 in 100. If your child has coeliac disease and eats food containing gluten, the gluten damages the lining of the small intestine, which can cause symptoms including vomiting, diarrhoea, stomach pains, smelly stools and a bloated tummy. It also means they will have problems absorbing essential nutrients such as calcium or iron. The good news is that as soon as you remove gluten from your child's diet the symptoms can disappear completely. However, your child will need to follow a gluten-free diet for life – it's not something they will grow out of.

It's important to explain to your child why they can't eat certain foods, for example, because they will cause a bad tummy ache – and make sure there is always an alternative, such as rice noodles instead of normal pasta. Wheat-free and gluten-free baking can be a pleasure once you have learned to use and feel at home with the ingredients.

* Add slightly more liquid to your recipes because it will be quickly absorbed (and doesn't mean tough pastry as there is no gluten).

* You can substitute wheat-free and gluten-free flours for plain flour in many of my recipes, but there are always going to be some that just don't work with gluten-free flour. My advice is that it is generally best to substitute when there is a low ratio of flour to other ingredients as then you are less reliant on gluten in flour to hold the mixture together.

* Rice flour, polenta, buckwheat flour and potato flour are fine for coeliacs.

* For cakes, make sure you use non-stick tins that are well greased and lined on the base for easier turning out – gluten-free baked goods are always, by nature, a little more fragile.

* Many processed foods such as fish fingers or chicken nuggets contain gluten, and some use bread or wheat starch as fillers, so don't give your child any processed foods unless they are labelled gluten-free.

* Corn or rice-based cereals are fine.

* Crushed cornflakes will make a good coating for chicken nuggets or goujons of fish. I also have a recipe in the fish chapter for popcorn-coated fish, which is also gluten-free (see Crunchy Popcorn Fish, page 83). Crushed plain crisps are also an option. Or you could use a coating of gluten-free flour, egg and gluten-free breadcrumbs.

* Where a recipe calls for plain flour, mix 1 teaspoon of gluten-free baking powder to each 150 g (5½ oz) of gluten- or wheat-free flour.

* Where a recipe calls for self-raising flour, mix 3–4 level teaspoons of gluten-free baking powder to every 225 g (8 oz) of gluten- or wheat-free flour.

* I find that pastry holds together much better if you mix it with egg rather than just water – the egg helps to act as a binder.

* You may find it easier to roll pastry between two sheets of baking parchment. If you are making lots of gluten-free pastry, it is worth investing in a silicone rolling mat, which makes handling a lot easier.

grace's dairy & gluten-free bircher muesli

It's a good idea to steer your child away from eating only sugary, refined cereals. Try making your own delicious mueslis – you can customize these by mixing in your child's favourite fruits. If your child suffers from food allergies, you could substitute buckwheat flakes for the rolled oats and soya yoghurt for the natural yoghurt.

200 g (7 oz) buckwheat flakes or rolled oats
350 ml (12 fl oz) apple juice
2 apples
50 g (2 oz) sugar-free dried apple, chopped
125 g (4 oz) natural yoghurt or soya yoghurt
100 g (3½ oz) seasonal berries, such as raspberries and blueberries

* Put the buckwheat flakes or oats in a large mixing bowl and pour over the apple juice to cover them. Cover the bowl and leave in the fridge to soak overnight.
* In the morning, peel and grate the apples and add to the oat or buckwheat mixture. Stir in the dried apple and yoghurt. Spoon the mixture into bowls. Scatter the berries over each helping and serve immediately.

☆ For a gluten-free variation, use buckwheat flakes instead of the rolled oats. Alternatively, you could try quinoa flakes, but you will need an extra 150 ml (5 fl oz) apple juice.

cheesey mini quiches

PASTRY

165 g (6 oz) rice flour

55 g (2 oz) potato flour

2 tsp xanthan gum

⅓ tsp salt

a pinch of cayenne pepper

110 g (4 oz) cold butter, diced

55 g (2 oz) mature/sharp Cheddar, grated

2 tbsp freshly grated Parmesan

1 medium egg, lightly beaten

FILLING

3 tbsp drained canned sweetcorn

2 spring onions, finely sliced

1 medium tomato, seeded and diced

120 ml (4½ fl oz) milk

1 medium egg plus 1 egg yolk, lightly beaten

salt and pepper, to season

∗ To make the pastry, sift together the flours, xanthan gum, salt and cayenne pepper. Rub in the butter until the mixture looks like sand, then stir in the two cheeses. Add the egg and mix to a dough, adding a few drops of cold water if necessary. (Or pulse the dry ingredients 8–9 times in a food processor before adding the egg; then process until a ball of dough forms on the blades.)

∗ Roll out to 5-mm/¼-in thickness and cut out circles using a 9-cm (3½-in) cutter. Gently lift the circles into the cups of a non-stick muffin tin. Re-roll trimmings and cut to make a total of 12 quiches. If any cracks appear then patch with small pieces of pastry. Chill for 30 minutes, until the pastry is firm.

∗ Pre-heat the oven to 180°C/350°F/Gas 4. Divide the sweetcorn, spring onions and tomato among the pastry cases. Put the milk and eggs in a jug, and whisk to combine thoroughly then season. Pour the egg mixture into the pastry cases, being careful not to over fill. Bake for 20–25 minutes, until the filling is slightly puffed and the pastry is golden. Allow to cool in the tin for 10 minutes.

∗ Carefully remove the tarts from the tin and cool on a wire rack. Transfer to the fridge as soon as possible, if not eating immediately. If cooking from frozen, defrost overnight in fridge. Warm through in a low oven before eating.

chicken and leek pie with potato pastry

You need the mashed potato for this pastry to be fairly dry. To achieve this, it is a good idea to drain the cooked potatoes and allow them to sit in a colander for 10 minutes, until all of the steam has evaporated, before mashing them without any butter or milk.

FILLING

2 tbsp butter

1 small onion, chopped

1 medium leek, cleaned and sliced

450 g (1 lb) chicken thighs, cut into 2-cm (¾-in) cubes

400 ml (14 fl oz) chicken stock

2 tbsp cornflour, mixed with 2 tbsp cold water

4 tbsp double cream

PASTRY

150 g (5½ oz) cold mashed potatoes

50 g (2 oz) cornflour

75 g (2½ oz) rice flour

½ tsp salt

100 g (3½ oz) cold butter, coarsely grated (pop in freezer for 10 minutes to make it easier to grate)

2 tbsp water

1 egg, beaten, to glaze

* Melt the butter in a large pan and cook the onion and leek over a low heat for around 10 minutes, until translucent. Add the chicken and stock, bring to a simmer and cook for 6 minutes then stir in the cornflour paste and cook for around 2 minutes, until the sauce thickens. Remove from the heat, add the cream and season to taste with salt and pepper. Transfer to 4 small pie dishes with a lip, or one 20-cm (8-in) pie plate. Cool and chill.
* To make the pastry, mix potato, flours and salt together in a large bowl. Add butter and work in with your hands, then add enough of the water to mix to a smooth dough. (Or place all ingredients in a food processor and whiz to a dough.)

* Pre-heat the oven to 200°C/400°F/Gas 6. For the small pies, divide the dough into 4 and pat out circles big enough to cover the mini pie dishes. Place the pastry over the pie dishes and seal by crimping the edges with a fork. Chill for 1 hour or until the pastry is firm.

* For the large pie, put the dough on to a piece of cling film and pat or roll out to a 20 cm (8-in) circle the same size as the pie plate. Lift the cling film and pastry on to a plate or baking sheet and chill for 1 hour until firm. Carefully flip the pastry over on to the top of the pie plate (it may help to flip it on to the palm of your hand and then slide on to the pie plate) and peel off the cling film. Seal pastry to the pie plate by crimping with a fork or your fingers. Carefully press any cracks together to seal.

* Brush the top(s) of the pie(s) with beaten egg and cut a small steam hole in the centre using a sharp knife. Bake for 30 minutes (small) or 45–50 minutes (large) until the top of the pie is golden and the filling is hot.

cheesey choux puffs

These small puffs are crisp and cheesey outside, light inside and delicious served with a tomato dipping sauce.

40 g (1½ oz) potato flour
80 g (3 oz) rice flour
½ tsp xanthan gum
¼ tsp salt
120 ml (4 fl oz) cold water
55 g (2 oz) cold butter, cubed
2 medium eggs
55 g (2 oz) Cheddar, grated
1 tbsp freshly grated Parmesan, plus 1 tbsp extra for sprinkling (optional)

* Sift together the flours, xanthan gum and salt twice, and transfer to a piece of baking parchment with a sharp crease in the centre. The parchment will help you to form a chute so that you can easily funnel the flour into the pan later.
* Put the water and butter in a medium pan over a medium heat. Allow the butter to melt then bring to a boil for a few seconds. Remove the pan from the heat and funnel the flour into the pan. Immediately beat with a wooden spoon until the mixture forms a ball. Transfer to a large bowl and allow to cool for 10 minutes.
* Beat the eggs into the flour mixture, one at a time, using a wooden spoon, followed by the Cheddar and Parmesan. The choux paste will now store in the fridge for up to 2 days, with cling film pressed on the surface.
* Pre-heat the oven to 200°C/400°F/Gas 6. Spoon the choux paste on to lightly oiled baking sheets, and sprinkle with extra Parmesan (if using).
* Bake without opening the oven door for the first 20 minutes. Small puffs should be firm and browned on the outside after 20 minutes. Large puffs need 25 minutes. Remove from the oven and cut in half. Scoop out the soft centre and discard and return the shells to the oven for a further 5 minutes, until crisp. To serve as rolls, bake for 30 minutes and retain centres.
* Store in an airtight tin for 1 day or freeze and defrost at room temperature for around 2 hours. Reheat in a 200°C/400°F/Gas 6 oven for 5–10 minutes.

flourless peanut butter and chocolate chip cookies

Peanut butter with chocolate is always a winning combination for fussy eaters. These cookies taste so good that you will never know they are made without flour.

235 g (8¼ oz) smooth peanut butter, at room temperature
165 g (6 oz) caster sugar
1 medium egg
¼ tsp bicarbonate of soda
a large pinch of salt
165 g (6 oz) milk chocolate chips (or milk chocolate, chopped)

* Pre-heat the oven to 180°C/350°F/Gas 4.
* Put the peanut butter, sugar, egg, bicarbonate of soda and salt in a large bowl and mix with a wooden spoon until thoroughly combined. Mix in the chocolate chips.
* Take rounded tablespoons of the mixture and roll into balls. It helps to dip the spoon in water every couple of cookies. Put the balls on baking sheets, spaced 5 cm (2 in) apart. Flatten the balls slightly with your fingers and bake for 12–15 minutes. The cookies should have spread out to around ½ cm (⅙ in) thick and have a slightly cracked surface.
* Allow the cookies to cool on the baking sheet for 10 minutes before carefully transferring to a wire rack, using a spatula or palette knife. Cool thoroughly and store in an airtight tin for up to 3 days or freeze. If frozen, defrost by spreading out on a baking sheet or plate at room temperature for 30 minutes.

PREPARATION TIME 25 MINUTES, PLUS CHILLING
COOKING TIME 15 MINUTES
MAKES 4 MINI PIZZAS
SUITABLE FOR FREEZING

polenta mini pizzas

Polenta is golden-yellow cornmeal made from ground maize.
The instant or quick-cook powdered variety can be made in minutes
and if you flavour it with vegetable stock and Parmesan it tastes
delicious. Cut into circles, it makes a good base for pizzas. Leftover
polenta can be cut into squares or triangles and baked as a side dish,
or coated in gluten-free flour mixed with Parmesan and fried.

BASE
750 ml (1¼ pints) hot vegetable stock
190 g (7 oz) instant polenta
60 g (2½ oz) freshly grated Parmesan
salt and pepper, to season

TOPPING
4 tbsp Annabel's Secret Tomato Sauce (page 45) or a jar of pasta sauce
60 g (2½ oz) Cheddar or mozzarella, grated
toppings of your choice, such as strips of ham, pepper or tomato

* Bring the vegetable stock to the boil in a large pan and pour in the polenta
in a thin stream, whisking constantly. Cook, stirring, until the polenta is thick
– around 3–5 minutes. Remove from the heat and stir in the Parmesan and salt
and pepper to taste. Spread the polenta out on a lightly oiled baking sheet to
around 5-mm (¼-in) thickness. Leave to cool then chill until set – around 1 hour.
* Pre-heat oven to 200°C/400°F/Gas 6. Cut out 4 large circles using a 9-cm (3½-in)
cutter. (Alternatively cut the base into a pretty shape, like the flower-shaped one
in the photograph.) Top each pizza with 1 tablespoonful of sauce and some
grated cheese. Add any other toppings that you like. Transfer the pizzas to a
lightly oiled baking sheet and bake for 13–15 minutes, until the cheese is bubbling.
* You can freeze these pizzas already assembled and bake from frozen, adding
2–3 minutes to the cooking time.

polenta mini pizzas

TOPPINGS
Another good topping for the polenta base is caramelized red onion, flavoured with balsamic vinegar and thyme and then topped with melted cheese.

The perfect lemon polenta cake

It can be hard to find a truly delicious cake that doesn't contain any flour. Yes, you can buy gluten-free cakes but sadly I find them disappointing. When it came to writing this chapter there was one cake I just had to include, and so I rang Ruth Rogers and Rose Gray of the River Café to see if I could include their wonderful polenta cake – this recipe comes from the original *River Café Cookbook*. I am sure many children, regardless of whether they suffer a wheat allergy or not, will be very grateful.

450 g (1 lb) unsalted butter, softened
450 g (1 lb) caster sugar
450 g (1 lb) almonds, ground
2 tsp vanilla extract
6 eggs
grated zest of 4 lemons
juice of 1 lemon
225 g (8 oz) polenta
1 tsp baking powder
½ tsp salt
gluten-free flour for dusting

* Pre-heat the oven to 160°C/300°F/Gas 3. Butter and flour a 30-cm (12-in) round cake tin.
* Using an electric mixer, beat the butter and sugar together until pale and light. Stir in the ground almonds and vanilla. Beat in the eggs, one at a time. Fold in the lemon zest and juice, polenta, baking powder and salt.
* Spoon into the prepared tin and bake for 45–50 minutes or until set. The cake will be brown on top. Serve on its own or with ice cream.

gluten-free brownies

These gooey, chewy brownies are so good that you will love them whether you have a gluten allergy or not. You can replace half of the white chocolate with roughly chopped pecans. These are also excellent served as a dessert with vanilla ice cream.

200 g (7 oz) plain chocolate, cut into chunks
200 g (7 oz) butter, cut into 1-cm (½-in) chunks
3 large eggs
175 g (6 oz) light muscovado sugar
110 g (4 oz) gluten-free plain flour
3 tbsp cocoa powder
2 tsp gluten-free baking powder
a pinch of salt
150 g (5½ oz) white chocolate, chopped
icing sugar, for dusting (optional)

* Pre-heat the oven to 160°C/300°F/Gas 2. Put the chocolate and butter in a heatproof bowl over a pan of simmering water and stir until melted. Alternatively, put the chocolate and butter into a suitable bowl, microwave for 1 minute, stir then microwave in 10-second blasts until melted. Allow to cool slightly.
* Using an electric mixer, whisk the eggs and sugar together until just combined. Stir in the chocolate and then sift and fold in the flour, cocoa powder, baking powder and a large pinch of salt. Fold in the white-chocolate chunks.
* Line a 28 cm × 20 cm (11 in × 8 in) cake tin with baking parchment, with the parchment coming up the sides of the tin. Pour the mixture into the tin and bake for 30 minutes, until a crust has formed but there is some give underneath when pressed. Do not overbake. Remove from the oven and allow to cool thoroughly in the tin – don't worry, it will sink and crack a little.
* Remove from the tin and cut into squares before serving. You can dust with icing sugar if you wish.

cranberry and white chocolate cookies

You can't compare shop-bought biscuits to home-made cookies. This combination of cranberry and white chocolate is a real winner. I tend not to add nuts when making cookies for fussy children, because a lot of children refuse to eat anything with nuts in it, but for adults it's good to add 50 g (2 oz) chopped pecans.

125 g (4½ oz) lightly salted butter, softened
150 g (5½ oz) soft light brown sugar
1 large egg, lightly beaten
½ tsp vanilla extract
150 g (5½ oz) gluten-free plain white flour (Doves Farm is the one most widely available), sifted
1 tsp gluten-free baking powder
100 g (3½ oz) white chocolate, chopped into chunks
50 g (2 oz) dried cranberries
1½–2 tbsp water

* Pre-heat the oven to 200°C/400°F/Gas 6. Line 2–3 baking sheets with baking parchment.
* In a mixing bowl, beat the butter and sugar together using an electric mixer or a wooden spoon until pale and creamy. Add the egg and vanilla extract a little at a time and continue beating until thoroughly combined.
* Stir in the flour, baking powder, white chocolate, cranberries and water and mix until thoroughly combined. Place tablespoons of the mixture on to the baking sheets, leaving plenty of space as they will spread in the oven.
* Bake for 15 minutes or until golden. Remove from the oven and allow to cool on the baking sheet for 2–3 minutes, then place on cooling racks.
* Store in an airtight container.

☆ The mixture is quite soft when you put it on to the baking sheets, and the cookies are soft when they first come out of the oven, but when they cool down they will harden. This is a good recipe for children to make with you as it's so quick and easy to prepare.

blueberry muffins

Blueberries are enjoyed by many children and these blueberry muffins are popular at breakfast or for tea. The soured cream makes them nice and moist.

250 g (9 oz) gluten-free plain flour
a large pinch of salt
1 tbsp gluten-free baking powder
180 g (6 oz) caster sugar
125 g (4½ oz) blueberries
2 large eggs
180 ml (6 fl oz) sunflower oil
180 ml (6 fl oz) soured cream
1 tsp vanilla extract
juice and grated zest of 1 small lemon

* Pre-heat the oven to 190°C/375°F/Gas 5.
* Stir together the flour, salt, baking powder, sugar and blueberries. Whisk together the eggs, oil, soured cream, vanilla extract, lemon juice and zest (it will look a bit curdled). Stir the wet ingredients into the dry ingredients and spoon into 12 muffin cases until about three-quarters full.
* Bake for 20–25 minutes. Allow to cool in the tin for 5 minutes before removing. Best served warm, though you can keep for a day in an airtight tin or freeze.

☆ A bowl of blueberries makes a good snack. According to researchers at the University of Boston, they top the list in terms of antioxidant activity when compared with 40 other fresh fruit and vegetables. While containing well-known antioxidants, such as vitamins C and E, their main health benefits come from the pigment (anthocyanin) that gives blueberries their blue colour.

wheat-free birthday cake

Coeliacs can feel particularly left out at birthday time without a cake and candle. You can either fill it with jam and vanilla buttercream or use the chocolate buttercream.

300 g (10½ oz) gluten-free plain flour
a large pinch of salt
1 tbsp gluten-free baking powder
140 g (5 oz) unsalted butter, melted
200 ml (7 fl oz) milk
150 ml (5 fl oz) sunflower oil
350 g (12 oz) caster sugar
4 medium eggs
2 tsp pure vanilla extract
1½ tbsp icing sugar, for dusting

FILLING
100 g (3½ oz) butter, at room temperature
175 g (6 oz) icing sugar, sifted
½ tsp vanilla extract
1 tbsp milk
4–5 tbsp raspberry jam

CHOCOLATE BUTTERCREAM
60 g (2 oz) plain chocolate, melted
100 g (3½ oz) butter, at room temperature
165 g (6 oz) icing sugar
1 tbsp milk

* Pre-heat the oven to 180°C/350°F/Gas 4. Grease and line two 20-cm (8-in) round baking tins. Sift together the flour, salt and baking powder. Mix together the melted butter, milk and sunflower oil.
* Whisk the sugar, eggs and vanilla extract together until pale and frothy. Whisk in one third of the oil-and-milk mixture followed by one-third of the sifted flour. Repeat twice. Pour into the cake tins (the mixture will be very liquid). As the mixture is so liquid you may like to put a baking sheet on the rack underneath the cakes to catch any drips.

* Bake in the oven for 40–45 minutes, until a skewer inserted into the centre comes out clean. Cool for 10 minutes in the tins, then turn out the cakes. Cool thoroughly on a wire rack and peel off the lining paper.

* To make the filling, beat the butter until pale and fluffy and beat in the icing sugar a little at a time. Beat in the vanilla and the milk a teaspoonful at a time until the buttercream is spreadable (you may not need all the milk). Spread jam over one side of the cake and spread the buttercream on top. Cover this with the other half of the cake and dust with icing sugar.

* To make the chocolate buttercream, first break the chocolate into pieces and melt in a heatproof bowl over a pan of simmering water. Alternatively, melt in the microwave. Allow to cool down a little. Beat the butter until pale and fluffy and beat in the icing sugar a little at a time. Fold in the melted chocolate followed by the milk

PREPARATION TIME 15 MINUTES
COOKING TIME 25 MINUTES
MAKES 8
SUITABLE FOR FREEZING

vanilla fairy cakes

It's just no fun if you go to a birthday party and can't eat any of the cakes, so here's a recipe that doesn't contain gluten but produces deliciously light little fairy cakes.

100 g (3½ oz) butter, at room temperature
100 g (3½ oz) golden caster sugar
2 large eggs, preferably room temperature
55 g (2 oz) gluten-free plain flour
55 g (2 oz) ground almonds
1 tsp gluten-free baking powder
a pinch of salt
1 tsp vanilla extract

* Pre-heat the oven to 180°C/350°F/Gas 4.
* Beat the butter and sugar until pale and fluffy. Add the remaining ingredients and mix to combine.

* Spoon into 8 cake liners in a muffin tin and bake for 20–25 minutes, until risen and firm to the touch. Cool for 5 minutes in the tin, then transfer to a rack until cold.

* You can ice these with buttercream (see Birthday Cake recipe, opposite) or glacé icing made from icing sugar and a little warm water. Store in an airtight tin for up to 5 days or freeze (un-iced).

Cookies and cakes

trail mix bars

Trail mix is a snack food commonly used in outdoor recreational activities such as hiking, backpacking and mountaineering. It usually consists of a mixture of nuts, seeds and dried fruits such as raisins and cranberries. It's energy rich and has a high content of vitamins and minerals. Fussy eaters often eat more between meals than they do at mealtimes, so it's important to give them healthy snacks such as these bars rather than letting them graze on empty calories that will spoil their appetite for their main meal.

55 g (2 oz) butter
3 tbsp golden syrup or clear honey
100 g (3½ oz) quick-cook oats
80 g (3 oz) packed soft brown sugar
30 g (1 oz) Cheerios
40 g (1½ oz) raisins
40 g (1½ oz) salted peanuts or pumpkin seeds
55 g (2 oz) milk chocolate chips or dried cranberries
35 g (1¼ oz) sunflower seeds
¼ tsp salt

* Pre-heat oven to 170°C/325°F/Gas 3. Line a 20 cm × 20 cm (8 in × 8 in) tin with baking parchment and grease lightly.
* Put the butter and golden syrup in a small pan over a low heat until the butter has melted. Set aside to cool.
* Put the remaining ingredients in a large bowl and stir together. Add the cooled butter mixture and mix well to combine. Transfer the mixture to the prepared tin and press down firmly. Bake for 30–35 minutes until the centre is just firm to the touch.
* Remove from the oven, cool for 15 minutes then mark into 8 bars, using a sharp knife. Allow to cool completely before lifting from the pan. Store in an airtight container.

carrot spice cookies with maple fudge glaze

If you love carrot cake then this is the cookie for you. With oats and carrots, this is a cookie with at least a few healthy ingredients that you can sneak past a fussy eater. If you make these cookies without the glaze, increase the sugar to 100 g (3½ oz).

100 g (3½ oz) butter, melted and cooled
75 g (2½ oz) golden caster sugar
1 egg yolk
75 g (2½ oz) plain flour
1½ tsp mixed spice
½ tsp salt
100 g (3½ oz) rolled oats
2 medium carrots, grated
50 g (1¾ oz) raisins

MAPLE FUDGE GLAZE
75 g (2½ oz) icing sugar, sifted
15 g (½ oz) butter, melted
3 tbsp maple syrup
2–4 tbsp milk

* Pre-heat the oven to 180°C/350°F/Gas 4. Line three large baking sheets with parchment paper.
* Mix together the butter, sugar and egg yolk. In a large bowl combine the flour, mixed spice, salt, oats, carrots and raisins. Pour on the butter and stir until well combined.
* Take tablespoons of the dough and roll into walnut-sized balls. Put on the baking sheet and flatten slightly (to 2 cm/¾-in thick). Bake for 20–25 minutes or until golden, rotating the baking sheets halfway through. Cool on a wire rack.
* To make the glaze, mix together the icing sugar, melted butter, maple syrup and 2 tablespoons of the milk. If the glaze is too thick (it should coat the back of a spoon in a thin layer) then add more milk, a teaspoon at a time. Dip the tops of the cooled cookies in the icing, allowing the excess to drip off. Leave on a rack to dry for 30 minutes.
* Store in an airtight tin for up to 3 days.

carrot bar cake

Big portions can be off-putting for fussy eaters, so I have opted to turn the traditional round carrot cake into a bar cake that is more suitable for cutting into kid-friendly fingers.

200 g (7 oz) plain flour
2 tsp baking powder
¼ tsp bicarbonate of soda
1 tsp ground cinnamon
1 tsp ground ginger
½ tsp salt
140 g (5 oz) drained canned pineapple chunks or rings
3 medium carrots, grated
140 g (5 oz) caster sugar
100 ml (3½ fl oz) sunflower oil
3 large eggs
85 g (3 oz) raisins (optional)

ICING
175 g (6 oz) full-fat soft cheese, at room temperature
100 g (3½ oz) unsalted butter, at room temperature
45 g (1½ oz) icing sugar
2 tbsp maple syrup

* Pre-heat the oven to 180°C/350°F/Gas 4. Line a 19 cm × 28 cm (7 in × 11 in) rectangular cake tin with baking parchment and grease with a little oil.
* Put all the cake ingredients (except for the raisins) in a food processor. If your processor has a grating disc, then use this to grate the carrot into the bowl of the food processor. Switch the blade and just add all the other ingredients (except the raisins). Whiz for 1–1½ minutes to make a batter. At this point you can stir in the raisins if using.
* Bake for 30–35 minutes or until firm to the touch and a skewer inserted in the centre of the cake comes out clean. Cool in the tin for 15 minutes, then turn out on to a wire rack and cool thoroughly before icing.
* When it comes to icing the cake, it is important that everything is at room temperature, otherwise the butter and soft cheese won't blend properly. Beat together the butter and cheese until smooth. Beat in the icing sugar and maple syrup and spread over the cake. Cut into squares before serving.

my favourite ginger biscuits

These delicious, slightly chewy ginger biscuits are great fun to make, as children love rolling out dough and cutting it into shapes using cookie cutters.

65 g (2 oz) butter, at room temperature
50 g (1¾ oz) soft brown sugar
4 tbsp golden syrup
150 g (5½ oz) plain flour, sieved
1 tsp ground ginger
½ tsp bicarbonate of soda
ICING
225 g (8 oz) icing sugar
2–3 tbsp water
edible silver balls, to decorate (optional)

* Beat the butter, sugar and golden syrup with an electric whisk until pale. Add the flour, ginger and bicarbonate of soda and beat together until you form a dough. Wrap in cling film and chill for at least 30 minutes until firm.
* Pre-heat the oven to 180°C/350°F/Gas 4.
* Roll out the dough on a floured work surface to a thickness of about 3 mm (⅛ in). Start in the centre of the dough and roll evenly outwards. (You can do this between two sheets of baking paper if the dough is still very soft.) Cut into shapes using cookie cutters, working from the outside edges of the dough into the centre, cutting as close together as possible. Re-roll the trimmings until all the dough is used up.
* Place on baking sheets lined with baking paper and bake for about 8 minutes. Allow to cool then transfer to a wire rack to cool completely.
* To make the icing, sift the icing sugar into a bowl, gradually beat in just enough water to give a smooth icing that is thick enough to pipe. Cut greaseproof paper into 15–18-cm (6–7-in) squares then cut in half to make triangles. Roll up the triangles to make cones and fold over the paper at the open end to secure. Pipe white icing on to the cookies to decorate them, and if you like you could add some edible silver balls.

my favourite ginger biscuits

TIP:
Children love icing biscuits themselves – encourage them to make different animal characters like bears and rabbits.

jamaican banana muffins

The smell of these baking should lure many children into the kitchen, eager for the crisp cinnamon crust and moist banana muffin underneath. For maximum flavour make sure that you use very ripe bananas.

75 ml (2½ fl oz) sunflower oil
100 g (3½ oz) light muscovado sugar
250 g (9 oz) very ripe bananas (unpeeled weight), mashed
1 medium egg
140 g (5 oz) self-raising flour
20 g (¾ oz) wholemeal flour
½ tsp salt
½ tsp bicarbonate of soda
½ tbsp ground cinnamon
3 tbsp very hot water
75 g (2½ oz) raisins

TOPPING
1 teaspoon ground cinnamon
60 g (2¼ oz) granulated sugar
10 g (½ oz) butter, melted

* Pre-heat the oven to 180°C/350°F/Gas 4.
* Mix together the sunflower oil and sugar. Add the mashed bananas and mix thoroughly. Beat the egg with a fork, add to the banana mixture and mix well.
* Sift the flours, salt, bicarbonate of soda and ground cinnamon into a medium-sized bowl. Tip in the little bits that were sieved out of the wholemeal flour. Add half the flour mixture to the banana mixture and mix well. Add the hot water and mix in thoroughly. Mix in the remaining flour and the raisins.
* Line a muffin tin with 8 paper cases and divide the mixture among them.
* Combine the topping ingredients in a small bowl and sprinkle evenly over the muffins. Bake for 25–30 minutes or until the muffins are well risen and spring back gently when you press the tops. Transfer to a wire rack to cool.

☆ For a gluten-free version: use 60 g (2¼ oz) sunflower oil, 160 g (5¾ oz) gluten-free flour, 1 tsp bicarbonate of soda and 2 tbsp hot milk instead of water. Bake for 30–35 minutes.

yoghurt pot fairy cakes

Children will love helping to make this recipe, as much of the measuring is done with one yoghurt pot.

1 × 125 ml pot natural full-fat yoghurt
2 pots plain flour (150 g/5½ oz)
½ tbsp baking powder
a pinch of salt
1 egg, lightly beaten
1 pot caster sugar (120 g/4 oz)
¾ pot (95 ml/3½ fl oz) sunflower oil
60 g (2 oz) dried apricot, chopped
1 tsp vanilla extract
15 g (½ oz) desiccated coconut

APRICOT BUTTERCREAM

1 tbsp apricot glaze or 3 tbsp apricot jam plus 1 tbsp water
150 g (5½ oz) butter, at room temperature
a few drops of vanilla essence
4 tbsp icing sugar
edible sugar flowers, to decorate (optional)

* Pre-heat oven to 180°C/350°F/Gas 4. Line a muffin tray with 12 fairy-cake cases.
* Scoop the yoghurt out of the pot into a large bowl. Rinse the pot out and dry it well. Use the pot to measure 2 pots plain flour and put this in a separate bowl with the baking powder and salt.
* Add the beaten egg to the yoghurt, along with one pot of sugar, then measure and add the ¾ pot sunflower oil. Stir in the chopped apricots. Stir in the vanilla, followed by the flour mixture. Finally fold in the coconut. Spoon the batter into the cake cases and bake for approximately 20 minutes, until risen, golden and firm to the touch. Cool for 10 minutes in the tin then transfer to a wire rack to cool completely.
* To make the buttercream, beat together the apricot glaze, softened butter and a few drops of vanilla essence then beat in the icing sugar. If you can't find apricot glaze, heat 3 tablespoons of apricot jam in a saucepan together with a tablespoon of water, sieve and leave to cool before use.
* Ice the top of each cake and decorate, if you like, with an edible sugar flower. Store in an airtight tin for up to five days.

oat, apple and sunflower seed muffins

Muffins make a good snack as you can sneak in healthy ingredients, and they make good portable food.

285 g (10 oz) plain flour
150 g (5½ oz) light muscovado sugar
2 tsp baking powder
½ tsp salt
1 tsp ground ginger
½ tsp mixed spice
50 g (2 oz) rolled oats
2 medium eating apples, core removed, chopped into small dice
20 g (¾ oz) sunflower **seeds**
50 g (2 oz) raisins
110 ml (4 fl oz) sunflower oil
4 tbsp golden syrup
2 medium eggs, lightly beaten
170 ml (6 fl oz) milk

TOPPING
20 g (¾ oz) rolled oats
20 g (¾ oz) sunflower seeds
20 g (¾ oz) demerara sugar

* Pre-heat oven to 200°C/400°F/Gas 6. Line a muffin tin with 12 muffin cases.
* Sift the flour, sugar, baking powder, salt, ginger and mixed spice into a large bowl, rubbing any lumps of sugar through the sieve. Stir in the oats, apples, sunflower seeds and raisins.
* Whisk together the oil, syrup, eggs and milk until thoroughly combined, then stir into the dry ingredients. Spoon into the muffin cases.
* Stir together the topping ingredients and divide among the muffins. Bake for 20–22 minutes, until risen and firm to the touch. Cool in the tin then transfer to a wire rack to cool completely. Keep in an airtight container for up to three days.

PREPARATION TIME 15 MINUTES
COOKING TIME 25 MINUTES
MAKES 8 PORTIONS
SUITABLE FOR FREEZING

chocolate puddings with chocolate fudge sauce

Always a favourite in my house. Even the fussiest of eaters wouldn't say no to this!

CHOCOLATE SPONGE

125 g (4½ oz) butter, at room temperature, plus 1 tbsp extra for greasing

125 g (4½ oz) soft light brown sugar

3 large eggs, lightly beaten

100 g (3½ oz) plain flour

25 g (1 oz) cocoa powder

2 tsp baking powder

¼ tsp salt

75 g (2½ oz) plain chocolate, chopped

CHOCOLATE FUDGE SAUCE

100 g (3½ oz) plain chocolate, chopped

4 tbsp soft light brown sugar

2 tbsp golden syrup

20 g (¾ oz) butter

200 ml (7 fl oz) double cream

vanilla ice cream, to serve

* Pre-heat the oven to 180°C/350°F/Gas 4. Grease 8 small pudding basins and line bases with circles of baking parchment.
* Cream the butter and sugar until fluffy. Add the eggs and sift over the flour, cocoa, baking powder and salt and beat until just combined. Fold in the chopped chocolate.
* Spoon the batter into the prepared basins (to half full). Bake for 20 minutes until risen and firm to the touch. Allow to cool slightly, then turn out the puddings (you may need to run a knife around the edge).
* To make the fudge sauce, put all of the ingredients in a medium pan and heat gently until smooth. Bring to a boil then remove from the heat and pour over the warm puddings. Serve with vanilla ice cream.

☆ You could also bake the chocolate sponge in a 20 cm × 20 cm (8 in × 8 in) cake tin lined with parchment. Baking time may be a bit longer (30–35 minutes). Cut into squares and serve with the chocolate sauce.

PREPARATION TIME 8 MINUTES
COOKING TIME 10 MINUTES
MAKES 18
SUITABLE FOR FREEZING

anzac biscuits

There are a few theories on the origins of Anzac biscuits but it is certain that they were first made during the First World War, around 1914–15. 'Anzac' stands for Australia and New Zealand Army Corp. Some say they started as biscuits made by the troops in the trenches with provisions they had to hand to relieve the boredom of their wartime rations. Others say they were made by resourceful women on the home front who wanted a snack that would keep well during naval transportation to loved ones fighting overseas. The beauty of these biscuits is that they are incredibly simple to make – a good recipe for getting your child involved in the kitchen.

85 g (3 oz) porridge oats
85 g (3 oz) desiccated coconut
100 g (3½ oz) caster or brown sugar
100 g (3½ oz) plain flour
a pinch of salt
100 g (3½ oz) butter, plus extra for greasing
1 tbsp golden syrup
1 tsp bicarbonate of soda
2 tbsp boiling water

* Grease a couple of baking trays and preheat the oven to 180°C/350°F/Gas 4. Mix the oats, coconut, sugar, flour and salt in a large bowl. Melt the butter in a small pan and stir in the golden syrup. Add the bicarbonate of soda to the boiling water and stir this into the golden syrup mixture.
* Make a well in the centre of the dry ingredients and pour in the golden syrup mixture. Stir well. Put dessertpoons of the mixture onto the greased baking trays, flatten the tops slightly and place at least 2.5 cm (1 in) apart to allow room for spreading.
* Bake for about 10 minutes or until golden. Leave for a few minutes to firm up before transferring to a wire rack to cool.

egg-free oat and raisin cookies

There is nothing quite like an egg, especially when it comes to baking. Egg protein is the magical ingredient that holds cookies together and creates light, fluffy sponge cakes. Unfortunately, egg protein is also a potent allergen. Egg replacers designed mainly for cake-making are one solution and can be found in some health-food stores and specialist suppliers. But they can't mimic the rich flavour that eggs give to cakes, so you may need to add extra butter or flavourings like vanilla. These cookies are quite delicious without egg.

85 g (3 oz) butter, at room temperature
75 g (2½ oz) soft brown sugar
1 tbsp golden syrup
1 tsp vanilla extract
50 g (2 oz) plain flour
75 g (2½ oz) rolled oats
¼ tsp bicarbonate soda
½ tsp salt
75 g (2½ oz) raisins
50 g (2 oz) pine nuts or sunflower seeds

* Pre-heat the oven to 180°C/350°F/Gas 4.
* Cream the butter, sugar and golden syrup together until pale and fluffy then beat in the vanilla. In a separate bowl, stir together the flour, oats, bicarbonate of soda and salt then fold into the butter mixture, followed by the raisins and pine nuts or sunflower seeds.
* Take roughly 2 tablespoons and roll into a golf-ball size. Put on lightly greased baking sheets, spaced around 4 cm (1½ in) apart, and flatten slightly.
* Bake for 12 minutes, rotating the baking sheets halfway through. Remove from the oven and allow to cool on the baking sheets for about 12 minutes or until lightly golden, then carefully transfer to a cooling rack and allow to cool thoroughly. The cookies will become more crisp as they cool.
* Store in an airtight container for up to five days.

PREPARATION TIME 12 MINUTES
COOKING TIME 20 MINUTES (PLUS CHILLING TIME)
MAKES 8 CUPCAKES
SUITABLE FOR FREEZING (UN-ICED)

ultimate chocolate cupcakes

Fussy eaters are guaranteed to like chocolate, and these are deliciously chocolatey but at the same time light and fluffy.

55 g (2 oz) plain chocolate

55 g (2 oz) butter, at room temperature

65 g (2¼ oz) dark brown sugar

1 large egg, beaten

½ tsp vanilla extract

4 tbsp soured cream

55 g (2 oz) plain flour

1 tbsp cocoa powder

½ tsp baking powder

a large pinch of salt

WHITE-CHOCOLATE BUTTERCREAM ICING

75 g (2½ oz) white chocolate

75 g (2½ oz) butter, at room temperature

2 tbsp icing sugar

2–3 drops vanilla extract

a pinch of salt

30 g (1 oz) milk chocolate, grated, for decoration (optional)

* Pre-heat oven to 180°C/350°F/Gas 4. Line a muffin tin with 8 cake cases.
* Melt the plain chocolate over a pan of hot water and allow to cool for 5 minutes. Cream the butter and brown sugar in a bowl until fluffy then beat in the cooled chocolate, followed by the egg, vanilla and soured cream. Sift the flour, cocoa and baking powders and a large pinch of salt, into the bowl and fold in.
* Spoon into the cake cases (around two-thirds full). Bake for 18–20 minutes, until risen and firm to the touch. Cool thoroughly on a wire rack.
* Melt the white chocolate over a pan of warm water and allow to cool for 5 minutes. Beat the butter, sugar and vanilla together with a pinch of salt then beat in the cooled chocolate. Chill for 20–30 minutes, stirring every 10 minutes, until firmer but still spreadable. Swirl the frosting over the cakes and chill for around an hour, until the icing has set. You can grate a little milk chocolate over the cakes just before serving.

heaven-sent chocolate cake

This cake takes only a few minutes to prepare in a food processor and it is deliciously moist. It's also a fun cake for children to prepare themselves. Chocolate is not all bad as it contains iron, calcium and potassium plus a variety of vitamins.

25 g (1 oz) cocoa powder
60 ml (2 fl oz) boiling water
200 g (7 oz) soft margarine
200 g (7 oz) caster sugar
4 eggs
200 g (7 oz) self-raising flour
2 tsp baking powder

CHOCOLATE MOUSSE ICING
200 g (7 oz) good-quality plain chocolate
2 tbsp dark rum or 1 tsp imitation rum flavouring
1 × 142 ml carton sour cream
1 × 284 ml carton double cream
1 Cadbury's Chocolate Flake, Smarties or Mini Eggs

* Pre-heat oven to 180°C/350°F/Gas 4. Grease and line two 20 cm (8 in) sandwich tins.
* Stir the cocoa powder into the boiling water until dissolved. Pour into the bowl of an electric mixer and add the margarine, sugar, eggs, flour and baking powder and beat for 2 to 3 minutes. Divide the mixture in half and spoon into the prepared tins. Bake for about 20 minutes or until risen and a cocktail stick inserted in the centre comes out clean. Allow to cool, then turn out on to a wire rack.
* Meanwhile, prepare the icing. Melt the chocolate and rum together with 4 tablespoons of the sour cream in a heatproof bowl set over a pan of simmering water, and stir until just melted. Remove from the heat, allow to cool a little and stir in the remaining sour cream. Set aside for about 10 minutes to cool down. Whip the double cream until it forms soft peaks and fold into the chocolate mixture.
* Spread half the icing over one of the cakes and place the second cake on top. Spread the remaining icing over the top and sides of the cakes and then sprinkle the top with a crushed Cadbury's Flake, Smarties or Mini Eggs. Set aside in the fridge for several hours until the icing is firm.

animal fairy cakes

Fairy cakes are always popular for tea or for a children's party, and it's fun to decorate them to look like animals, in this case, rabbits and chicks.

140 g (5 oz) butter, well softened
140 g (5 oz) golden caster sugar
3 medium eggs
1 tsp pure vanilla extract
125 g (4½ oz) self-raising flour
GLACÉ ICING
175 g (6 oz) icing sugar, sieved
about 2 tbsp water
yellow food colouring
DECORATION
100 g (4 oz) ready-to-roll white icing
pink food colouring
Liquorice Allsorts, Jelly Tots, Jelly Diamonds

* Pre-heat the oven to 190°C/375°F/Gas 5. Line a bun or muffin tray with 10 paper cases.
* Put all the ingredients for the sponge into a mixing bowl and beat for about 2 minutes until smooth. Divide the mixture among the paper cases so they are filled two-thirds of the way up. Bake for approximately 18–20 minutes until risen and lightly golden or until a cocktail stick inserted in the centre comes out clean.
* Mix the icing sugar with enough water to form a spreading consistency, then divide into two and colour one half yellow, using a couple of drops of yellow food colouring. Transfer to a wire rack to cool.
* Colour one-third of the ready-to-roll white icing with pink food colouring. Make 6 pairs of rabbit ears, using some of the white and some of the pink icing.
* Cover half the cakes with the white icing and half with the yellow icing. Add the ears to the white rabbit cupcakes. Decorate using Liquorice Allsorts and Jelly Tots. Decorate the yellow-iced chicks with Jelly Tots and Jelly Diamonds. Store in an airtight container for up to two days.

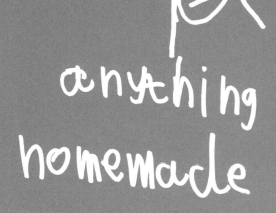

i don't like...

anything
homemade

hummingbird cupcakes

Deliciously moist cupcakes. You could use drained cubed pineapple in this recipe (using one 227-g can) and just put everything in a food processor and blitz. You could then put any leftover pineapple on top. These can be served with or without the topping.

110 g (4 oz) plain flour
1 tsp baking powder
¼ tsp bicarbonate of soda
1 tsp ground ginger
¼ tsp salt
30 g (1 oz) shredded coconut
100 g (3½ oz) soft light brown sugar
1 medium egg, beaten
100 ml (3 fl oz) sunflower oil
115 g (4 oz) drained crushed pineapple (half a 432-g can)
1 large, ripe banana, mashed

TOPPING
110 g (4 oz) full-fat soft cheese, at room temperature
110 g (4 oz) butter, at room temperature
4 tbsp icing sugar
3–4 drops vanilla extract
2 tbsp drained crushed pineapple, to decorate

∗ Pre-heat oven to 180°C/350°F/Gas 4. Line a muffin tin with 8 paper cases.
∗ Stir together the flour, baking powder, bicarbonate of soda, ginger, salt, shredded coconut and sugar. Beat the egg and oil together and add to the dry ingredients, along with the pineapple and banana. Stir together quickly and spoon into the paper cases. Bake for 20–25 minutes, until the tops are firm to the touch. Cool on a wire rack.
∗ To make the topping, beat together the soft cheese, butter, sugar and vanilla extract. Spread over the cupcakes and chill until firm. Top with a little pineapple just before serving. Store in the fridge.

PREPARATION TIME 25 MINUTES
COOKING TIME 25 MINUTES
MAKES 7–8 PORTIONS
SPONGE SUITABLE FOR FREEZING

sticky toffee pudding

Good old-fashioned comfort food is generally popular as pudding for fussy eaters, and you can't go wrong with this recipe. The sponge and sauce can be made in advance. The sponge also freezes well. Simply defrost, arrange the sponge on a serving plate, pour over some sauce and re-heat in a microwave (on High) or re-heat in the oven, as below, and warm the sauce in a pan.

PUDDING
55 g (2 oz) unsalted butter
170 g (6 oz) demerara sugar
1 tbsp golden syrup
1½ tbsp black treacle
2 eggs
200 g (7 oz) self-raising flour
290 ml (10 fl oz) boiling water
200 g (7 oz) pitted dates
1 tbsp bicarbonate of soda
½ tsp vanilla extract
vanilla ice cream, to serve

FOR THE MOULDS
25 g (1 oz) butter, softened
25 g (1 oz) flour

TOFFEE SAUCE
100 g (3½ oz) butter
100 g (3½ oz) soft brown sugar
200 ml (7 fl oz) double cream
a few drops of vanilla extract
a pinch of salt

* Pre-heat the oven to 180°C/350°F/Gas 4. Butter 7 or 8 pudding moulds and dust with flour.
* Cream the butter and sugar together in a food processor. Gradually add the golden syrup, treacle and eggs. Continue to mix until smooth, then turn down the speed and add the flour, making sure everything is well mixed in.
* Pour the boiling water over the dates and blitz in a blender. Stir in the bicarbonate of soda and the vanilla. Pour the date purée into the batter while still hot and stir well. Divide the mixture between individual pudding moulds, and bake for 20–25 minutes until the tops are just firm to the touch.
* To make the sauce, melt the butter and sugar together in a pan. Add the cream, vanilla and a pinch of salt. Bring to the boil, stirring a few times, then simmer for 1 minute.
* Remove the puddings from the moulds. Place each one on a plate, coat with the warm sauce and serve with a scoop of vanilla ice cream.

fruity finishes

how to get your child to eat fruit

* Whole fruit in a fruit bowl tends not to get eaten, but how about arranging a plate of colourful cut-up fruit for when your child gets home from school or even thread some bite-sized pieces of fruit onto a straw or a skewer.

* Make sure that any fruit you serve is fully ripe – taste it yourself. Serving unripe, tasteless fruit can put children off.

* Try making fresh-fruit ice lollies by blending fresh fruit and mixing with fruit juice or yoghurt, then freezing in ice lolly moulds.

* Find fun ways of serving fruit, like making melon balls; or cut kiwi fruit in half and serve in an egg cup. Make a mango hedgehog by cutting the flesh into diagonal cubes and turning inside-out.

* Buy a liquidizer and encourage your child to make his own smoothies. In cold weather, serve hot fruity puddings like rhubarb-and-pear crumble.

* Encourage your child to make his own freshly squeezed orange juice by using an electric orange squeezer.

* Introduce lots of variety – exotic fruits are more readily available in supermarkets so introduce your child to stoned lychees, passion fruit, mango or pomegranate.

* Make tasty muffins using fruits like banana or apple and get your child to help make them. Mini muffins are popular so it's a good idea to buy a mini muffin tray and bake both large and small muffins.

* Add fruit to your child's cereal or make your own delicious granola and add dried fruits.

* Always include some fresh fruit in your child's lunchbox. Make sure it is easy to eat so peel fruits such as clementines and wrap in cling film, and give wedges of melon, mango etc.

* When you go out, take something fruity with you, such as grapes, a small banana or dried fruit for when your child is hungry.

Children love jelly and combining it with fruit is another good way to up their fruit intake

PREPARATION TIME 10 MINUTES
(PLUS CHILLING)
MAKES 4 PORTIONS

PREPARATION TIME 10 MINUTES
COOKING TIME 10 MINUTES
MAKES 2 PORTIONS

elderflower jelly

You could use a mixture of berry fruits instead of the peaches, pear and grapes. If you have never used leaf gelatine, you will be surprised how it dissolves perfectly every time, so now making jelly is really easy. You can buy leaf gelatine in most supermarkets.

300 ml (10 fl oz) elderflower cordial
400 ml (14 fl oz) cold water
6 leaves gelatine
1 tsp fresh lemon juice
125 g (4½ oz) mixed fruit, e.g. chopped peaches (canned or fresh), a tin of fruit cocktail, or a mixture of berry fruits

* Mix the cordial with the cold water in a jug. Soak the gelatine for 5 minutes in just enough cold water to cover. Meanwhile, warm 100 ml (3 fl oz) of the cordial mix in a medium pan until hot but not boiling. Remove from the heat.
* Squeeze out any excess water from the gelatine. Stir the gelatine into the warm cordial until fully dissolved. Add the remaining cordial mix and the lemon juice, and stir well. You must add the remaining cordial to the dissolved gelatine and not vice versa, or it can cause the gelatine to go stringy.
* Divide the fruit among 4 small glasses and pour in the cordial mix. Chill overnight.

apples with toffee sauce

This goes well served warm with vanilla ice cream or rice pudding or cold with thick Greek yoghurt. Alternatively, you could use it as a filling for pancakes (see pages 28–9). A delectable combination of warm caramelized fruit with melting cold vanilla ice cream.

2 medium apples
15 g (½ oz) butter
45 g (1½ oz) caster sugar
4 tbsp double cream
4 drops vanilla extract
a pinch of salt

* Peel and core the apples and cut into 12 chunks. Melt the butter, add the sugar and cook until it turns to light caramel (4–5 minutes).
* Stir in the cream and apples, and simmer for 3–4 minutes or until the apples are tender. Remove from the heat and stir in the vanilla and salt.

fruit salad with passion fruit syrup

Sadly, whole fruit in a fruit bowl rarely gets eaten. This lovely fruit salad is a good way to tempt fussy eaters.

3 passion fruit (look for wrinkly passion fruit – this means they are ripe)
60 g (2 oz) sugar
2 tbsp water
2 tsp fresh lime juice
1 medium mango, peeled, stone removed, cut into cubes
½ small pineapple, peeled, cored and cubed
1 papaya, seeded, peeled and diced

* Scoop the seeds and pulp from the passion fruit into a sieve. Push through as much juice as possible (approximately 60 ml/2 fl oz). Put in a small pan with the sugar and water and stir over a low heat until the sugar has dissolved. Bring to the boil and cook for 30 seconds. Cool and add the lime juice.
* Put the fruit in a large bowl and pour over the passion-fruit syrup. Allow to stand for 30 minutes before serving.

☆ Try to give your child a wide variety of fruits, as different fruits provide different nutrients. For example, a single kiwi fruit supplies more than the normal daily requirement of vitamin C for an adult, while mango is a very rich source of beta-carotene (vitamin A), which is essential for growth, healthy skin, fighting infection, and good vision. It may seem obvious, but if you want your child to enjoy eating fruit, do make sure the fruit is ripe. Other fruits you could add are stoned lychees or cantaloupe melon, which looks good if you scoop out the flesh using a melon baller.

apple and blackberry crumble

Crumbles are surprisingly easy to make as you can whiz up the topping in a food processor – take care not to over-mix. Alternatively, children might have more fun helping you make the topping by hand.

40 g (1½ oz) butter
900 g (2 lb) eating apples (e.g. Gala, Pink Lady, Fuji), peeled, cored and sliced about ½-cm (¼ in) thick
2½ tbsp soft light brown sugar
350 g (12 oz) fresh or frozen blackberries
CRUMBLE TOPPING
225 g (8 oz) plain flour
a good pinch of salt
1 tsp ground cinnamon
110 g (4 oz) cold butter, cubed
100 g (3½ oz) caster sugar
3 tbsp soft light brown sugar

* You will need a 21 cm × 16 cm (8 in × 6 in) ovenproof dish.
* Pre-heat the oven to 200°C/400°F/Gas 6.
* Melt the butter in a large pan and sauté the apples for 1 minute. Sprinkle over the sugar and continue to cook for 2 minutes more. Stir in the blackberries. Spoon the fruit into the ovenproof dish.
* To make the crumble topping, mix together the flour, salt and half a teaspoon of the cinnamon and rub in the butter, then stir in the sugar. Alternatively, whiz together in a food processor for a few seconds.
* Sprinkle the crumble topping over the fruit. Mix the remaining cinnamon with the brown sugar and sprinkle over the crumble topping. Bake for 40 minutes.

annabel's berry mess

Meringue tends to be popular with children, so try combining it with berry fruits – the combination of slightly tart berries with crushed meringue is heavenly. Berries are very rich in vitamin C, which helps us to fight infection and absorb iron. You could also purée and sieve some raspberries together with a little icing sugar to make a raspberry coulis and stir this through the mixture. Making raspberry coulis is another way to boost your child's vitamin-C levels, and it goes well with vanilla ice cream and peaches to make a peach melba.

260 g (9 oz) mixed berries (e.g. blueberries, blackberries, strawberries, raspberries)
1 tbsp plus 1 tsp icing sugar
125 ml (4 fl oz) double cream
¼ tsp vanilla extract
1 × 200 g pot thick Greek yoghurt
2 meringue nests, broken into small pieces

* Put the berries in a bowl. Add 1 tablespoon of icing sugar and mix, crushing a few of the berries. In a separate bowl, put the cream, 1 teaspoon of icing sugar and the vanilla, and whip to soft peaks.
* Stir the yoghurt to loosen slightly then carefully fold into the cream, followed by the berries and the meringue pieces. Spoon the mixture into 4 glasses and serve.
* You can chill this for up to 30 minutes but not much longer otherwise the meringue will start to go soggy.

annabel's berry ~~mess~~ mess

TIP:
When children cook they learn skills like counting, measuring, weighing and understanding time – all without noticing.

mini meringue pavlova

Pavlova is a meringue dessert named after ballet dancer
Anna Pavlova. The meringue is crisp on the outside but chewy
on the inside. It's very popular with children and fun for them
to make themselves.

MERINGUE
2 large egg whites
½ tsp cornflour
½ tsp fresh lemon juice
a pinch of salt
100 g (3½ oz) caster sugar

TOPPING
100 g (3½ oz) raspberries, plus extra for decoration
1½ tbsp icing sugar
6 tbsp mascarpone cheese
mint leaves (optional), for decoration

* Pre-heat the oven to 120°C/230°F/Gas ½.
* Cut a piece of baking parchment to fit a large baking sheet. Draw 6 × 10-cm
(4-in) diameter circles on the paper (use a large cup or ramekin as a template)
and put the parchment on the baking sheet, pen-side down, so you don't get
ink on the meringue.
* Whisk the egg whites with the cornflour, lemon juice and salt until the
mixture reaches stiff peaks. Sprinkle over one-third of the sugar and whisk
until it reaches stiff peaks again. Repeat with another third of the sugar then
whisk in the final third of sugar.
* Spoon the meringue into the centre of the circles and spread out, using the
circles as a guide. Alternatively use an ice-cream scoop to form six circles. Make
a little indentation in the centre of each using the back of a teaspoon. Bake for
approximately 50 minutes until crisp on the outside and dry underneath. Cool,
then gently peel off the paper.
* Mash the raspberries with the icing sugar. Stir half into the mascarpone, then
ripple through the remaining raspberries. Spoon a little of the mixture into the
middle of the meringues and decorate with extra raspberries and maybe a
couple of mint leaves.

rhubarb and pear crumble

If your child isn't keen on eating fruit, you might be able to tempt him or her with this fruity crumble – it's one of my favourites. Rhubarb is great for making crumble, as the slightly tart fruit combines well with the sweet crumble topping. And, hey, a little secret – strictly speaking rhubarb is a vegetable and so you have managed to get your child to eat fruit and vegetables. I put ground almonds into the dish before I add the fruit as this helps to soak up some of the juices and stop the crumble from becoming soggy.

25 g (1 oz) butter
½ tsp ground ginger
4 tbsp demerara sugar
4 ripe pears, peeled, cored and cut into chunks
400 g (14 oz) rhubarb, cut into 2 cm (½ in) pieces
2 tbsp ground almonds

CRUMBLE TOPPING
50 g (2 oz) rolled oats
100 g (3½ oz) plain flour
55 g (2 oz) amaretti biscuits, crumbled
85 g (3 oz) unsalted butter, cut into cubes
55 g (2 oz) demerara sugar
a large pinch of salt

* Pre-heat the oven to 200°C/400°F/Gas 6. Melt the butter in a large pan, add the ginger and sugar and allow to dissolve. Add the pear and cook on a low heat for 2 minutes until softened. Stir in the rhubarb and cook for 2 minutes. Sprinkle the base of an ovenproof dish (or several individual dishes) with the ground almonds and spoon the fruit on top.
* To make the topping put the oats, flour, amaretti biscuits and a large pinch of salt in the bowl of a food processor and whiz into crumbs. Add the butter and pulse until it has disappeared, then add the sugar and pulse once or twice to combine.
* Spread the crumble over the top of the fruit and bake in the centre of the oven for about 35 minutes until lightly golden.

i don't like...

any
hot fruit

frozen berries with hot white-chocolate sauce

This is served up in some of the poshest restaurants as dessert, but it's dead simple to make at home and oh-so plate lickingly good that I defy the fussiest eater to refuse it! It's best to freeze the berries yourself, as ready-frozen berries tend to go a bit mushy when defrosted. This is a particular favourite of my daughter Lara, who has always been a bit fussy. She was the inspiration behind the 'I don't like...' lists in this book!

150 g (5½ oz) frozen mixed berries (e.g. blackberries, raspberries, blueberries, strawberries, redcurrants)
55 g (2 oz) white chocolate, chopped into small pieces
4 tbsp double cream

* To freeze the berries, line a rimmed baking sheet with parchment or greaseproof paper and arrange the berries in a single layer. When they are frozen, transfer to small freezer bags. They will last for 1 month and are also good in smoothies.
* Take the berries out of the freezer and divide between two bowls. Allow them to defrost slightly at room temperature for around 10 minutes.
* Put the chocolate and cream in a microwaveable jug and cook for 10 seconds, stir and repeat heating and stirring until chocolate has just melted (it will take 4–5 blasts) and you have a smooth sauce. Alternatively, put the cream and chocolate in a small bowl over a pan of simmering water and stir continuously until the chocolate has just melted.
* Pour the hot sauce immediately over the berries and serve at once.

knickerbocker glory

Let your child make up her own combination of jelly, fruit and ice cream. Simply use a packet of jelly if you don't have time to make your own.

1 × 500 ml (17 fl oz) tub good-quality vanilla ice cream

JELLY
6 sheets leaf gelatine
400 ml (14 fl oz) cranberry juice
3 tbsp caster sugar
200 ml (7 fl oz) lemonade

RASPBERRY SAUCE
180 g (6 oz) raspberries
2 tbsp icing sugar
½ tsp fresh lemon juice

PLUS TWO OR THREE OF THE FOLLOWING
3 ripe kiwi fruits, peeled and diced
200 g (7 oz) mixed berries
3 rings fresh or canned pineapple, diced
½ large ripe mango, peeled and diced
1 × 300 g can mandarins, drained

* To make the jelly, soak the gelatine leaves in cold water for 5 minutes. Meanwhile warm 100 ml (3½ fl oz) of the cranberry juice in a pan, add the sugar and place over a medium heat until hot but not boiling. Squeeze any excess water from the gelatine and stir into the warm cranberry juice, until dissolved. Allow this to cool for a few minutes, stir in the remaining juice and lemonade and pour into a bowl. Pop in the fridge and chill for 4–5 hours or overnight, until set. When set, you can chop some of the jelly into pieces.
* To make the sauce, blend the raspberries, icing sugar and lemon juice. Sieve to remove seeds and chill until needed.
* To construct the knickerbocker glories, take 4 sundae glasses and divide some of the jelly among each glass. Layer the fruit over the jelly. Add another layer of chopped jelly and top with scoops of ice cream. Finally, pour over the raspberry purée. Serve with long spoons.

ice lollies

What child can resist an ice lolly and it's so easy to make your own from good healthy ingredients like puréed fruits, fruit juice or yoghurt. You could simply freeze your child's favourite juice or fruit smoothie in ice lolly moulds. If you have time you could freeze in two stages using contrasting colours to make a two-tone ice lolly. Simply pour in the strawberry mix up to halfway, then freeze for a couple of hours and fill to the top with the tropical mix or simply use tropical fruit juice. Add the stick and when frozen you will have a red and orange lolly.

strawberry sorbet ice lollies

Most manufactured lollies are full of artificial flavouring and colouring so why not make your own from fresh fruit? Strawberries contain higher levels of vitamin C than any other berries.

30 g (1¼ oz) caster sugar
250 g (9 oz) strawberries, hulled and cut in half
juice of 1 medium orange (approx. 40 ml/ 2 fl oz)

* Put the sugar and 40 ml (2 fl oz) of water in a saucepan and boil until syrupy (about 3 minutes). Allow to cool.
* Purée the strawberries with an electric hand blender and combine with the cooled syrup and orange juice, then pour this mixture into the ice lolly moulds. Freeze until solid.

tropical lollies

If there is one food that almost no child can resist it has to be an ice lolly. It's easy to make your own by puréeing fruits and mixing the purée with fruit juice or yoghurt. You could also simply freeze pure fruit juice or fruit smoothies in ice-lolly moulds.

1 large mango, stone removed, peeled and diced
180 ml (6 fl oz) tropical fruit juice
3 tbsp icing sugar
1 tbsp fresh lemon juice

* Blend the ingredients together until smooth. Pour into 4 large ice-lolly moulds and freeze.

index

# about the author

ANNABEL KARMEL is a best-selling author on nutrition and cooking for babies, children and families. A mother of three, she has been hugely influential in her imaginative approach to creating healthy food that also tastes good. Annabel was awarded an MBE in 2006 in the Queen's Birthday Honours List for her outstanding work in the field of child nutrition.

Her first book, *The Complete Baby and Toddler Meal Planner*, written in 1991, has become the definitive authoritative guide on feeding babies and children and has sold several million copies worldwide. She has written a further 14 books, ranging from *Superfoods for Babies and Children* to *Top 100 Baby Purées*, *Lunchboxes* and *Favourite Family Recipes*.

Annabel is the expert in getting your child, no matter how fussy, to eat a healthier diet – without them even noticing! She has developed tricks to get your children to improve their diet, from hiding vegetables in other foods, packing powerhouse lunchboxes and creating healthy junk food – without the need for parents to spend hours in the kitchen!

Annabel's recipe development expertise has enabled her to work with numerous manufacturers as a consultant, including Marks and Spencer.

In 2006 she launched 'Make Your Own...' with Boots, an innovative range of equipment and foods to help make it easy for mums to prepare their baby's meals. In 2007 she launched 'Eat Fussy', her own range of healthy chilled meals created especially for young children so that mums can serve their children proper food even when they don't have time to cook. She also launched a stylish range of feeding utensils designed to help babies progress from first tastes to feeding themselves.

Annabel writes regularly for national newspapers including *The Times*, *Mail* and *Sunday Mirror* as well as contributing to *Practical Parenting*, *BBC Good Food* and *Sainsbury's Magazine;* she is also the food expert for *Mother and Baby* magazine. She is the children's celebrity chef on the BBC website and also appears frequently on radio and television as the UK's expert on nutritional issues. Recently, she completed a series on Channel 4's *Richard and Judy Show* as the Foodie Godmother, where she travelled around the UK solving the problems of fussy eaters.

Visit www.annabelkarmel.com. It's packed with recipes and advice and is a great place to chat and network with other mums. Also visit www.annabelkarmel.tv where you can get lots of tips, advice and recipe videos.

author acknowledgments

Despite pleas of 'Please mum, can you finish experimenting before we bring our friends over?', I want to thank Nicholas, Lara and Scarlett and all their friends for testing my recipes.

Caroline Brewster, my good friend and runner-up in Masterchef 2005, for cooking up a storm with me in the kitchen.

Dave King, my absolutely fabulous photographer. For the fun times in the studio and his inimitable style and flair. This book wouldn't be the same without you.

Everyone at Ebury. Carey Smith for persisting in encouraging me to write this book in the first place. Sarah Lavelle for her hard work in putting the book together in record time. Fiona Macintyre for her enthusiasm and belief that it could be done. Sarah Bennie for telling everyone about it.

Evelyn Etkind, my mum, for stealing the finished recipes and inviting her friends over for supper.

A big thank you to all the gorgeous children who appear in the book. Yes, I know it's hard to smile, look happy and eat at the same time, but you were all wonderful: Aimee and Lucy Spencer, James Duggan, Lucy Pulver, Pareece Cooke, Oscar and Emily Lindopp, Phoebe Leary, James Farmery, Lily Wells, Sam Sheppard, and thanks to Vicky Orchard for organizing all the parents and children.

Helen Armitage, my editor, who not only dotted my i's and crossed my t's but also worked her way through cooking and eating my recipes, which was above and beyond the call of duty.

Tessa Evelegh for the stylish props.

Ben Tisdall of Taylor Herring. For being super-enthusiastic about the book and helping the world know all about it. Mary Jones, my PR, for always being the bearer of good news.

Elizabeth Jones for keeping the business running whilst I put on my pinny. My very own superwoman, you are much appreciated.

Jacqui Morley and David Karmel, for helping to bring some organization into my chaotic life.

Marina Magpoc and Letty Catada, for assisting me in testing the recipes

Everyone at Smith and Gilmour for patiently working with Dave and me to get the right look.

Ruth Rogers and Rose Gray for allowing me to reproduce the stunning Lemon Polenta Cake from their *River Café Cookbook*; and Grace Cheetham for her muesli and smoothie recipes from *The Best Gluten-Free, Wheat-Free and Dairy-Free Recipes*.

To Stephen, for his support and encouragement.

websites

www.annabelkarmel.com will give you the best advice and guidance on feeding your baby and child. Packed full of delicious and healthy recipes, nutritional advice and wonderful top tips for every stage and age. You can chat to other parents on my friendly community forum and in return get great support and recipe ideas.

More and more parents go online for advice, which is why I have launched annabelkarmel.tv the all new online internet TV channel! Here you can watch free videos that will give you my advice on food and nutrition for you and your little ones.

annabel karmel says
eat fussy

It's good to be a bit fussy about what you eat these days. That's why I have created a new range of tasty, yet healthy meals made especially for children. They're balanced, mouth-watering meals for young children aged 1 to 4 without the fuss. What's more, I'm very fussy about what goes into them so I only use the best natural ingredients.

- Scrummy Chicken Dumplings with Rice
- Mummy's Favourite Salmon and Cod Fish Pie
- Beef Cottage Pie
- Yummy Beef Lasagne
- Hidden Vegetable Pasta
- Cheeky Chicken and Potato Pie
- Teddy Bear Pizzas
- Meatballs with Spaghetti and Tomato Sauce

Look for **Eat Fussy** in the chilled section of your local supermarket: just ask!

annabel's berry ~~mess~~ mess

prawn toasts

i like...

polenta mini pizzas

strawberries and cream

Y